Practical Portfolios

Practical Portfolios
Reading, Writing, Math, and Life Skills, Grades 3–6

Susan B. Mundell
Karen DeLario

Illustrated by
John Brasaemle

1994
TEACHER IDEAS PRESS
A Division of
Libraries Unlimited, Inc.
Englewood, Colorado

To Our Class,
The Graduates of the Year 2000

Copyright © 1994 Susan B. Mundell and Karen DeLario
All Rights Reserved
Printed in the United States of America

No part of this publication may be reproduced, stored in a retrieval system, or transmitted, in any form or by any means, electronic, mechanical, photocopying, recording, or otherwise, without the prior written permission of the publisher. An exception is made for individual library media specialists and teachers who may make copies of activity sheets for classroom use in a single school. Other portions of the book (up to 15 pages) may be copied for in-service programs or other educational programs in a single school.

TEACHER IDEAS PRESS
A Division of
Libraries Unlimited, Inc.
P.O. Box 6633
Englewood, CO 80155-6633
1-800-237-6124

Library of Congress Cataloging-in-Publication Data

Mundell, Susan B.
   Practical portfolios : reading, writing, math, and life skills,
 grades 3-6 / Susan B. Mundell and Karen DeLario ; illustrated by
 John Brasaemle.
    vii, 149 p. 22x28 cm.
   Includes bibliographical references (p. 141) and indexes.
   ISBN 1-56308-197-0
   1. Portfolios in education--United States. 2. Education,
Elementary--United States. 3. Educational tests and measurements-
-United States. I. DeLario, Karen. II. Title.
LB1029.P67M86   1994
372.12'6--dc20   93-47183
                                                                                                 CIP

Contents

1—Introduction 1
   Introduction 1
   Traditional Assessment 1
   Portfolio Assessment 2
      Benefits of Portfolios to Students, Teachers, and Parents 4
      Whole-Child Portfolios and the Seven Intelligences 4
      Life Skills Training 5
      Outcome-Based/Standards-Based Education 6
   Student-Led Parent Conferences 6
   How to Use This Book 7
      Portfolio Components 8
      Overview of the Portfolio Lessons 9
      Student-Led Parent Conference Components 11
      Final Considerations 12
   Conclusion 12
      Questions About Portfolios 13
      Questions About Student-Led Parent Conferences 14
   Suggested Timelines 15
      Full School Year Timeline 16
      Modified Timeline 17

2—Getting Started 19
   Advance Preparations 19
      Student Supply Lists 19
      Classroom Supplies 19
      Classroom Setup 19
      Scheduling 20
   Lesson 1—Introducing the Portfolio and Choosing Covers 20
   Lesson 2—Decorating Covers 28
   Lesson 3—Assembling the Portfolios 28
   Lesson 4—Student Exit Outcomes 36
   Lesson 5—Student Illustrations of Exit Outcomes 38

3—Suggested First-of-the-Year Portfolio Lessons 40
   Lesson 6—Writing an Autobiographical Letter 40
   Lesson 7—Cooperative Learning 41
   Lesson 8—Creating a Classroom Rubric for Behavior Expectations 43
   Lesson 9—Self-Monitoring 50
   Lesson 10—Sharing Page 53
   Lesson 11—Learning Styles 57
   Lesson 12—Applications for Classroom Jobs 58
   Lesson 13—Interview Skills 60
   Lesson 14—Reading Survey 62
   Lesson 15—Writing Survey 64
   Lesson 16—Math Skills Demonstration 66
   Lesson 17—Computer Demonstration 68

4—Organizing Work into Portfolios, Writing Summaries, and Goals 69
    Lesson 18—Organizing First-of-the-Year Work into Portfolios and
        Making First VIP Entries 69
    Lesson 19—Creating a Classroom Rubric for Student Portfolios 72
    Lesson 20—First Writing Sample 74
    Lesson 21—Composing Reading and Writing Goals 82
    Lesson 22—Student Summary Writing for Life Skills and Math 87
    Lesson 23—Composing Life Skills and Math Goals 92
    Lesson 24—Reaching Your Goals 95

5—Fall Student-Led Parent Conferences 97
    Lesson 25—Introduction to Student-Led Parent Conferences 97
    Lesson 26—Introduction to the Fall Conference Agenda 100
    Lesson 27—Creating a Rubric for Student-Led Parent Conferences ... 102
    Lesson 28—Fall Conference Agenda Rehearsal 104
    Lesson 29—Continuing the Fall Conference Agenda Rehearsal 106
    Lesson 30—Practicing the Complete Agenda 106
    Lesson 31—Student Invitations to Parents 109
    Lesson 32—Student Thank-You Notes to Parents 110
    Lesson 33—Student Evaluation of Fall Conferences and Portfolios ... 110

6—Ongoing Portfolio Lessons 112
    Ongoing Portfolio Lessons 112
        Life Skills, Reading, Writing, and Math Sections 112
        Life Skills 112
        Writing 113
        Reading 113
        Math 113
        VIP 113
        Science and Social Studies 113
    Lesson 34—Completing the Exit Outcome Page 114

7—Sending the Portfolios Home 117
    Lesson 35—Sending the Portfolios Home 117

8—End-of-the-Year Portfolio Lessons 120
    Lesson 36—End-of-the-Year Writing Sample 120
    Lesson 37—End-of-the-Year Writing Survey 121
    Lesson 38—Writing Self-Reflections 121
    Lesson 39—End-of-the-Year Reading Survey 124
    Lesson 40—Adding Journal Entries and Reading Logs to the Portfolios 124
    Lesson 41—Reading Self-Reflections 125
    Lesson 42—Miscellaneous Activities 128

9—Spring Student-Led Parent Conferences 129
    Lesson 43—Spring Student-Led Parent Conferences 129
    Lesson 44—Completion of Exit Outcome Page for Second Semester 129
    Lesson 45—Introduction to the Spring Conference Agenda 132
    Lesson 46—Choosing a Math Manipulative 134
    Lesson 47—Selecting Science and Social Studies Activities 135
    Lesson 48—Spring Conference Agenda Rehearsal 135
    Lesson 49—Student Evaluation of Spring Conferences and Portfolios 137

References 141

Index 143

About the Authors 149

1 Introduction

INTRODUCTION

Today's student-centered classrooms, which emphasize process learning and authentic tasks, are quite different from those teacher-directed classrooms of the past. No longer is the teacher the all-knowing disseminator of information. Rather, the teacher is a guide and support, structuring lessons based on student needs.

The students also have different roles. Whereas students previously completed most assignments as directed by the teacher, in today's classrooms students make many of their own decisions about what to read and write, what math strategy to use, or how to best demonstrate their learning in a science or social studies project. By providing students with learning strategies and opportunities to make decisions, teachers are preparing students to become lifelong learners.

This book presents a practical approach to assessment and learning consistent with student-centered classrooms. However, before we discuss the components of the program and its use, we will summarize the current literature supporting the whole-child portfolio and student-led parent conference approach.

TRADITIONAL ASSESSMENT

Certainly, there are changes taking place in education; however, according to Tierney, Carter, and Desai (1991, 27–28), testing practices for reading and writing have changed little in almost 30 years. Traditionally, norm-referenced or standardized tests have been used to evaluate student performance. These tests measure growth in basic skills, and their content is based on the best of curriculum practices for a diverse population.

Norm referencing refers to how tests measure achievement based on the normal curve. On this curve, many students score around the 50th percentile on a test, with few students scoring very high or very low.

Most norm-referenced tests have a multiple-choice format. This makes the tests an easy and inexpensive way to evaluate knowledge.

According to the test manual for the Iowa Test of Basic Skills, there are many uses for the information obtained from these tests. These include reporting to parents on their children's progress in learning basic skills, determining the developmental levels of students for instructional purposes, and providing information helpful in planning programs or groupings for instruction. Diagnosis of group scores may indicate needed changes in instructional procedures and curriculum.

However, norm-referenced tests have several limitations considering the style of education today. First of all, standardized tests measure knowledge learned instead of showing what a student understands and can apply (Enoki 1992, 1). As stated by Tierney, Carter, and Desai, current research shows that understanding in reading comprehension and writing are based on students' experiences and purposes, but standardized tests still focus on recall. The how and why of what students read and write, the strategies they apply, and how this learning relates to other tasks and to new ideas are not measured (Tierney, Carter, and

Desai 1991, 28, 30). Stated another way, it is not possible to assess students' abilities to analyze, reason, reflect, and persuade from multiple-choice answers (Finn 1991, 167-68).

Also, the tests do not help teachers plan more effective lessons. If anything, the use of standardized tests limits the planning of lessons geared to students' needs. According to Finn, a school's curriculum objectives and the testing program seldom coincide. The result is that the test content is taught and studied (Finn 1991, 46, 161). Time spent preparing for and administering tests takes away from the already limited instructional time in the classroom (Tierney, Carter, and Desai 1991, 23).

Similarly, the students do not benefit directly from the tests. The students are subjects who participate in the testing, not for themselves, but because others have required it (Valencia 1990, 338). The students do not evaluate their work and then use the evaluations to further their learning (Tierney, Carter, and Desai 1991, 34).

In addition, the tests do not reflect the type of work being done in the classroom. This is apparent, for example, considering the way reading is taught in process-oriented classrooms. Trade books are used instead of basals, and response and discussion take the place of answering an established set of teacher questions. Journal and response activities are emphasized instead of workbook pages, and reading and writing are integrated. In most standardized test formats for reading, students read short passages in selected topics in which they may not have interest or background knowledge. Each test question has only one correct answer, and reading is tested separately from writing. Also, the tests do not take into account the value of the reading process (Tierney, Carter, and Desai 1991, 25, 27-28, 30). Then, too, the test questions are written by persons outside of the learning environments in which the tests are given.

Note that efforts have been made in Michigan and Illinois to develop norm-referenced reading tests that overcome some of the above problems. These tests take into account students' background knowledge in determining the comprehension score. The test passages are longer, and higher comprehension questions are included. Also, on the Illinois test, some questions allow for more than one possible answer. However, the tests still do not provide information about how students read in natural situations (Rhodes and Shanklin 1993, 374-77).

PORTFOLIO ASSESSMENT

Because of the inadequacies of standardized tests to help improve instruction and student performance, efforts have been made to develop methods of performance-based assessment. In performance-based assessment, students demonstrate through actual tasks what they know or are able to do. Portfolios, as assessment tools, developed out of this need to assess performance and to systematically gather samples of students' work (Enoki 1992, 5).

A portfolio is a collection of work that exemplifies an individual's expertise in an area, as an artist's portfolio contains various pieces showing what the artist can do. By adapting this idea for student assessment, a portfolio can be used to collect and evaluate multiple sources of information that show a student's competence in terms of process and product. The portfolio may contain a student's work in one or more subject areas, and the samples are selected by both the student and the teacher. The work samples are collected systematically over time and are used to measure student growth (Enoki 1992, 6-7).

There are many qualities of portfolios that make them useful as assessment tools. One of the characteristics is authenticity. For example, the teacher evaluates reading throughout a range of daily reading activities in the classroom. Students are evaluated on the reading strategies they demonstrate, their responses in their reading journals, and their discussion with the teacher or with peers. After all, assessing isolated subskills does not demonstrate what students do in authentic reading (Valencia 1990, 338). Also, actual writing that takes place in the classroom, whether stories, reports, journals, letters, or invitations, is used to demonstrate writing progress. Again, students may be able to demonstrate isolated writing skills and still not be able to write effectively.

Furthermore, portfolio assessment creates an accurate picture of achievement because it directly involves the teacher and students in establishing criteria for evaluation (Enoki 1992, 7). There is a direct correlation between what is studied and what is assessed, and students know from the start of an assignment what they are expected to achieve. Also, the students have several examples in their portfolios to demonstrate achievement of a particular goal, rather than just one sample taken during one testing situation.

Another characteristic of portfolio assessment is that students are evaluated against themselves, not compared with others (Taylor 1991, 4). Students learn to evaluate their skills and to set realistic goals. They can see their progress over time as skills are demonstrated on assignments and goals are achieved. This does not mean that there is no standard involved. An example is the Creative Writing Checklist on pages 78-81 (Jefferson County School District R-l, n.d.). The students' first stories of the year are evaluated by using the criteria on this checklist. If the students are at the beginning of fifth grade, they are not expected to show fifth-grade skills at this time. The teacher explains that the students are on different levels in the different categories, and that no matter what their current writing level, they are expected to show progress by the end of the year. Throughout the year, the teacher presents writing mini-lessons, the students continue to practice and develop writing skills on a variety of assignments, and the students continually achieve goals and write new ones. At the end of the year stories are again evaluated using the same criteria on the checklist. Evidence of success in writing is determined by growth demonstrated by each individual student, rather than by comparing the student with the group.

In portfolio assessment, evaluation is part of instruction (Enoki 1992, 7). Information is collected from work samples obtained during actual classroom lessons instead of taking instructional time to prepare for and do assessments. For example, during a writing conference, the teacher and student assess the piece of unfinished writing and determine that the student needs to learn to indent paragraphs. After individual instruction by the teacher and after class mini-lessons on paragraphing, the student works on this skill. When the student demonstrates understanding of paragraphing, the teacher and student may then decide that the student needs to learn to punctuate quotes. Evaluation and instruction continue, one leading to the other.

Another aspect of portfolio assessment is that it is ongoing. Not just the final product is important, but also the process and growth over time. The teacher may observe how well a student uses math problem-solving strategies in a variety of situations. Or perhaps a student struggling to learn the multiplication tables, although not yet at mastery, demonstrates growth by learning new facts each week. This ongoing assessment emphasizes to students and parents that learning is continuous and changing, something that is never truly finished (Valencia 1990, 338). To assure that assessment is ongoing, the teacher needs a timeline for selecting and evaluating portfolio entries throughout the year. This may be done weekly, quarterly, at the semester, or at the end of the school year.

Also, portfolio assessment is multidimensional. It takes into account students' interests, individual experiences, motivation, and strategies. These are aspects of instruction that teachers value and emphasize, but they are not measured by standardized tests (Valencia 1990, 338).

Finally, portfolio assessment is founded on joint reflection by teacher and student, who become partners in the educational process. Both play roles in evaluating the student's work, assessing strengths and weaknesses, and establishing goals. This process helps students become responsible for their own learning (Valencia 1990, 338).

Benefits of Portfolios to Students, Teachers, and Parents

Besides the advantages of portfolio assessment discussed above, there are other direct benefits to students. Students are more involved in the learning process. They better understand the criteria for evaluation, and they learn to evaluate their own work. They work harder on assignments because they recognize the importance of following the steps in the process instead of just working for a grade on the final project. This gives students more ownership in their work, increases their responsibility for their learning, and enhances their self-concepts as learners. Success is clearly demonstrated, and future successes can be built on present achievements. Also, the use of portfolios helps students develop critical thinking skills (Taylor 1991, 3-4, 18).

Teachers also benefit from portfolio use. Portfolios, by their structure, lead to better communication between teachers and students. They provide teachers with clear evidence of student achievement and show areas for improvement. Portfolios help teachers develop and revise instructional strategies to meet students' needs; teachers have to continually work to make criteria for assignments clearer. Thus, portfolios provide feedback for educators to assess their own teaching. The portfolios are helpful during conferences; student growth is demonstrated in ways that are understood by teachers, parents, and administrators (Taylor 1991, 4, 18). Portfolios may also serve as checks on other test results (Tierney, Carter, and Desai 1991, 51).

Parents also benefit when their children have portfolios of demonstrated performances. Parents can see what their children are actually achieving (Tierney, Carter, and Desai 1991, 51) and can better understand the curriculum and classroom expectations.

Whole-Child Portfolios and the Seven Intelligences

These research findings offer a convincing rationale in favor of portfolio assessment. However, pilot portfolio programs have concentrated on one or two subjects, such as reading and writing. A missing aspect in current portfolio development is an approach that will enable students, parents, and teachers to value and assess the whole child. The following discussion explains the advantages of implementing a whole-child portfolio as opposed to a narrowly focused one.

Portfolios that focus on one or two subjects ignore the fact that everyone has capabilities in many areas. Interested in these capabilities, Professor Howard Gardner of Harvard University launched a detailed study of intelligence. As a result, he concluded that people have at least seven intelligences, including linguistic, musical, logical/mathematical, spatial, bodily kinesthetic, intrapersonal, and interpersonal. All the intelligences are interrelated, and a person may excel in one of these seven areas but have capabilities in the other six (Gardner 1983, 77-78).

Linguistic intelligence indicates a special sensitivity to and understanding of the functions of language. It is the most widely shared of the intelligences. People excelling in this area recognize and have the ability to use language to convince, excite, stimulate, and convey information. An example of a professional who excels in this area of intelligence is a writer (Gardner 1983, 97).

The musical intelligence comprises a tremendous range of types and degrees of development. This intelligence is one of the earliest to emerge and involves an understanding of the elements of pitch and rhythm. Singers and composers are examples of professionals who have highly developed abilities in music (Gardner 1983, 99-122).

The ability to calculate and solve problems is characteristic of those with developed logical/mathematical intelligence. Any science or mathematical profession requires excellence in this area (Gardner 1983, 128-45).

Spatial intelligence is the capacity to perceive the visual world accurately and perform tasks and modifications based on that perception. Professional sculptors are just one example of those who use spatial intelligence in their work (Gardner 1983, 170–90).

Skillfully manipulating objects and controlling one's body are characteristics of those with high capabilities in the bodily kinesthetic intelligence. Many professions represent this intelligence, including acting, dancing, sports, and carpentry (Gardner 1983, 205–207).

The final two types are the personal intelligences: intrapersonal and interpersonal. They are tremendously important but often ignored or minimized. They relate to knowledge that revolves around self and others. Intrapersonal intelligence is characterized by an ability to access and understand one's own feelings. An author with the capability to write about deep emotions excels in this intelligence. Persons with developed interpersonal intelligence have an ability to notice and make distinctions among other individuals and their moods, temperaments, motivations, and intentions. Political and religious leaders, teachers, counselors, and therapists are all examples of professionals using this intelligence (Gardner 1983, 237–39).

Gardner took his research one step further when he examined IQ test scores. IQ tests generally measure knowledge, comprehension, and application—the three areas often taught and measured in the traditional classroom. He wanted to explore what correlation, if any, existed between IQ scores and academic performance. His findings revealed a high level of correlation between IQ scores and academic performance; however, there was no correlation between these scores and performance outside the classroom in real-life tasks and situations (Thornburg 1989, 91).

Gardner found that schools tend to teach the linguistic, logical/mathematical, and intrapersonal learners and to virtually ignore the other intelligences. This tendency has two negative consequences. First, the needs of children whose dominant intelligence is not one of these three are ignored. Second, the opportunity is lost to validate and develop the other intelligences in all children (Thornburg 1989, 92).

To avoid these pitfalls, it is necessary to design a method of teaching and assessing that encompasses the whole child. Indeed, this leads to the whole-child portfolio project in this book, with sections for all curriculum areas, as well as extracurricular and home activities. Schools today must prepare students for a wide range of professions, and this means including the full spectrum of the seven intelligences.

Life Skills Training

A commitment to teach, value, and assess the whole child is commendable but will only be effective if focused on skills needed in real life. Life skills are the requisite skills for surviving, living with others, and succeeding in a complex society (Hamburg 1990, 16). These skills often fall outside the current boundaries of traditional school curricula for several reasons.

In the past, future expectations were built into the family and extended-family experience in childhood. The lives that children knew and lived every day were very similar to the lives they would lead when they were grown. This simple transition to adulthood is no longer possible. Society is too complex, technology changes too quickly, and families do not have the time or expertise to give the life skills training needed. Children do not live and see the world in which they will be expected to survive (Hamburg 1990, 6).

This change in society has created a need for children and adolescents to find ways to develop visions of the future and to formulate images of what will be required of them in adulthood (Hamburg 1990, iii). The solution is to incorporate life skills training into everyday assessment and teaching. It follows that life skills should be an integral part of any portfolio system.

Through a whole-child portfolio that incorporates life skills, it is possible for children to see and understand, on a daily basis, the connection between what they are mastering in school and the real world. Assessment methods that have real-life validity encourage students to think about and solve real-life problems, rather than merely recite facts (Hearne and Schuman 1992, 12).

Outcome-Based/Standards-Based Education

Linking teaching, learning, and assessment to the whole child and basing it on real-life expectations has created a new look to high school graduation. Many school districts in North America are basing their graduation requirements on demonstrated skills rather than seat time. The terms outcome-based and standards-based education define these demonstrated skills. An analogy was given by Governor Roy Romer of Colorado, which brought these concepts into focus.

"I happen to be a pilot, and when I talk to people about national standards, I tell them that to become a pilot, there are certain things you need to know and be able to do. These things constitute criteria; they're outcome-based. It might take you 36 hours to meet these criteria and get a private license—or it might take you 46 hours. What is fixed is what you need to know. What is variable is how much time it takes you to learn" (Romer 1992, 36).

The planning of instructional activities begins with the exit outcomes describing the characteristics of a successful adult in the twenty-first century. (See examples on page 37.) These outcomes state in general terms the characteristics students should demonstrate upon graduation, focusing on preparation for future job markets. This focus is critical considering the changes in the work force over the past 40 years. In 1950, only 40 percent of positions were classified as professional, managerial, or skilled as compared to 65 percent in 1990. This percentage is predicted to increase to 85 percent by the year 2000 (Weber, 1993). It is critical that our schools move forward with the basic academics required of future workers, rather than back to the basics required by workers in the 1950s.

Although the exit outcomes are stated in general terms, students work toward the outcomes throughout their school careers by meeting well-defined guidelines for demonstrated skills at each grade level. The criteria to successfully demonstrate the skills is stated in the form of a rubric. A rubric is a set of descriptions used for classroom assessment purposes. It includes a standard and is used to evaluate the learner's performance. The descriptions are organized into four categories. "Novice" is severely below the standard, "emerging" is slightly below the standard, "standard" is the expected behavior for the proficiency, and "exceeds standard" goes beyond the standard (Dawson n.d.). It is beneficial to write rubrics in first person to foster increased student ownership (Vandamme 1992). (See pages 44-49, 61, 73, 103 for examples.)

By setting achievement standards rather than relying on a set amount of seat time, outcome-based education becomes a reality. Jefferson County Public Schools in Colorado started Education 2000 in 1989 to improve instruction and prepare students for the twenty-first century (Jefferson County School District R-1 1992, 1). The Harrison School District in Colorado Springs has also chosen to link graduation with outcome-based education. Students keep samples of their work in twenty-two item portfolios. A review of this portfolio system makes it readily apparent that the whole child is valued and assessed. Also noteworthy is the focus on life skills such as résumé writing and interview skills (Harrison School District 1992, 2, 95). Portfolios are clearly a part of the movement towards preparing students for the future with outcome-based education. It is not the intent of this book to provide detailed information on national standards and school reform. Teachers will need to seek the help of their school districts for additional information on this extensive topic.

STUDENT-LED PARENT CONFERENCES

We have shown that the portfolio is an effective vehicle for demonstrating performances in classrooms emphasizing process instruction. A format for students to present their portfolios to parents is the student-led parent conference. These conferences allow students, with training, to have the central role in reporting their progress to parents. Through these conferences, students learn organization and leadership skills. They become accountable for their learning, learn to evaluate their work, and develop communication skills (Little and Allan 1988, 11–12).

This is a change from traditional parent-teacher conferences. Although some students attend parent-teacher conferences, they seldom have active roles in the communication process. Parents often experience apprehension in the traditional conference format. This type of conference also does not help students become accountable or help teachers to motivate students (Little and Allan 1988, 6–7).

Little and Allan have presented a model for student-led parent conferences, which they state that many teachers prefer to hold in the spring. In their book, they outline several steps for teachers and students to follow. First, students make folders to hold the work samples to be shared with parents. Then students decide on the activities to be presented. Examples are a story to read, a math paper, a spelling list, and a science experiment or social studies project. The teacher prepares a conference agenda listing the activities in the desired order. The agenda is placed in the folder for the students to follow during the conference. A conference schedule is written, based on feedback from parents about desired times. Because the students are in charge of the conferences, several conferences take place in the room at one time. Next, the students write invitations to their parents, stating the scheduled time. The students rehearse for the conference, following the agenda and including introductions for the teacher and parents (Little and Allan 1988, 13–17).

At the conferences, the students present the activities and discuss the items with their parents according to the practiced agenda. The teacher circulates around the room, acting as a facilitator and providing support and encouragement. Students introduce the teacher and parents at appropriate times. Refreshments are served, the parents write notes to their children about their progress in school, and the students thank their parents for coming. As parents exit the conference room, they may write comments to the teacher about the conference. Parents also have the opportunity to request regular parent-teacher conferences to discuss special concerns. In their study, Little and Allan found that the student-led parent conferences met the needs of most parents, but that about three parents out of a class of 30 students would request a private conference with the teacher (Little and Allan 1988, 19–21, 29).

Following the conferences, the students write notes to thank their parents for coming. The students also evaluate the conferences in a class meeting (Little and Allan 1988, 22).

With the introduction of student-led parent conferences, the following results were noted: increased student ownership and accountability, improved parent-and-student communication, 92 percent to 96 percent parent attendance, more time for viewing and discussing progress in systematic detail, and an increased sense of pride on the part of the student (Little and Allan 1988, 24–28). Barbara Maughmer, an elementary school teacher in Manhattan, Kansas, enthusiastically stated that she had not found a better way to help students become self-confident and take responsibility for their own learning (Dismuke 1993, 13).

HOW TO USE THIS BOOK

In the following sections, we will explain the components of our portfolio and student-led parent conference format. In adapting these new approaches for our classroom, we have combined our own ideas with those of others to create a method of performance-based assessment that values the whole child. This method reflects the process-oriented classroom using the reading and writing workshop format.

Portfolio Components

As a regular classroom teacher and a special education teacher co-teaching in a fifth-grade class, we were interested in a portfolio format that emphasized the whole child by demonstrating growth and abilities in all curriculum areas as well as in activities outside of school. We also wanted a manageable format that we could put immediately into practice. Although there are currently many books and articles about the theory and basic practices of using portfolios, we found nothing available to meet our criteria. We decided that to have such a portfolio for our students we would need to create the format ourselves. We spent the 1992–93 school year developing our ideas.

This book was specifically designed to be teacher friendly. Clear, step-by-step directions are given for each lesson. Each one states the objective, gives suggestions for teacher preparation, and outlines specific lesson content. Included are portfolio components that can be photocopied, samples of letters home, and tips a teacher will need to create a successful portfolio and student-led parent conference program. Lessons can be modified, added, or omitted according to a teacher's individual teaching style. Items to be placed in the portfolio are not limited to the lessons presented in this book. Other suggestions of possible items are written on the title pages for each section. The entire project has been classroom tested. To provide guidance and clarification to students and teachers, many idea pages have been included to stimulate thinking. What teachers will notice, however, is that many current classroom activities will be appropriate for placement in the portfolio. An example is a story map completed by a student to meet requirements for a reading workshop assignment. The story map may be placed in the portfolio as a demonstration of reading comprehension.

The project is also student friendly. To help students visualize and remember the more difficult concepts, lessons use graphing and artwork when appropriate. In addition, two devices help students locate the correct area of the portfolio during mini-lessons. Pages relating to particular areas of the portfolio are color coded; for example, all teacher handouts relating to the Writing section may be green. Also, there is consistent use of symbols throughout the project, such as the picture of a pencil to indicate all pages that deal with the Writing section. The repetition of these symbols on the conference agendas enables students to keep their place better during student-led parent conferences. This is beneficial to all students but especially to those who have difficulty with reading.

The portfolio model we have developed has five sections: Life Skills, Reading, Writing, Math, and VIP (Very Important to this Person). Examples of items to be included in each section are written on the title pages. (See Life Skills, p. 30; Reading, p. 31; Writing, p. 32; Math, p. 33; and VIP, p. 35.) Three-ring notebooks with dividers are used for the portfolios. Such binders are sturdy for long-term use, and papers can be easily inserted or removed. Students decorate and personalize the portfolio covers, choosing from several cover designs included in this book or designing their own. An explanation of the portfolio concept is given on each portfolio cover.

The inside front pocket of the portfolio contains the Visitor Log. (See p. 29.) Persons viewing the portfolio are to sign it and make comments. The Visitor Log provides a record of how often and for what purpose visits are made. The log also serves as a reminder to everyone that the portfolio is to be used, not just placed on a shelf.

For the Life Skills, Reading, Writing, and Math sections, there is space on the title pages for summary writing. In this particular format, the teacher writes the summaries for Reading and Writing. The students write their summaries for the Life Skills and Math sections under the direction of the teacher and with examples furnished in this book. (See pp. 85, 86, 89, and 91.) Giving the students responsibility for writing the summaries of two portfolio sections allows them to reflect on and evaluate their own abilities and reduces the amount of teacher time required for maintaining the portfolios. On these pages, too, students write their goals for the different subjects. This summarized information and the accompanying goals are the basis for communication with parents about the students' achievements and current skills being emphasized. The students also complete the items for VIP. (See p. 71.) Through the mini-lessons presented in this book, the students become familiar with the portfolios and their role in the portfolio assessment process.

Parents also have input in the portfolios. They complete the Home Responsibility Inventory twice during the year. (See p. 27.) Through the student-led parent conferences, parents participate with their children in writing goals for Life Skills and adding items to the VIP section. They also write comments about their children's work in the Visitor Log.

Science and social studies do not have separate sections in the portfolio. Depending on the nature of the activity, a science or social studies item may apply to more than one section. Where it is placed is up to teacher or student discretion. For example, the written explanation of a science experiment about starch changing to sugar during digestion may go in Life Skills or in Writing. It applies to Life Skills because the experiment is an example of critical thinking, and it applies to Writing because it is a science report. Again, placing science and social studies activities into one of the existing sections streamlines the use of the portfolios, shows students how subjects are interrelated, and makes the portfolio easier to maintain. However, a teacher could certainly add sections for science and social studies if desired.

As stated previously, a timeline needs to be established to assure ongoing portfolio assessment. Two examples of timelines are included. (See pp. 15–18.) The first timeline gives a detailed overview to help teachers envision the whole project and how it fits into the school year. The second timeline is modified for teachers starting the portfolio project in the middle of the year.

Overview of the Portfolio Lessons

Information for getting started with portfolios is given in chapter 2. These lessons introduce students and parents to the portfolio concept. Each student selects and designs a cover and assembles the portfolio by placing the dividers, title pages, and a Visitor Log in the appropriate places in the notebook. The concept of outcome-based education is presented through the discussion of student exit outcomes (Jefferson County School District R-1 1992, 4–5). (See pp. 36–37.) Students make drawings representing the exit outcomes as visual symbols to help clarify meaning. (See pp. 38–39.) In this book, we have made the connection to outcome-based education wherever possible to help bring this concept into the classroom in practical, easy-to-understand activities.

The first-of-the-year lessons are in chapter 3. These lessons provide a profile of the whole child, giving the teacher information on the student's background and attitude. Although the lessons are arranged in a suggested order, this order can be easily modified. Included are an autobiographical letter written by the student to the teacher and an activity for cooperative learning. Behavior is addressed through the development of a rubric for behavior expectations and the use of self-monitoring pages (Wack and Effective Learning Resources n.d., 27–28). Sharing pages are provided to increase student awareness of self and others (Wack and Effective Learning Resources n.d., 4–16). Also in this chapter are the important life skills of completing an application, interviewing (Young Americans Education Foundation 1989, 18.1–18.3), and computer literacy. The reading and writing surveys are included because students' attitudes about subjects affect their motivation to learn (Atwell 1987, 270–72). The learning style lesson and math skills demonstration lesson provide additional information for the teacher as well as increased student self-awareness. All the activities in this chapter provide items to be inserted into the portfolio, and many of them serve as baselines for activities at the end of the year.

In chapter 4, students organize all completed work into the portfolios and make their first VIP entries. Students participate in creating a rubric for portfolio expectations. Lesson 20 outlines the procedures for evaluating the students' first writing samples according to the Creative Writing Checklist. The checklist provided in this book creates an awareness of the expectations for both teachers and students. However, teachers may use an evaluation tool that more closely reflects their district's guidelines for writing. For teachers using the provided checklist, a reproducible explanation is provided for visitors to the portfolio. This explanation helps visitors realize that the checklist is a general guideline to set expectations rather than to judge a student's writing as being good or poor. Students complete bar graphs to visually indicate their skill levels in different areas of writing. This baseline provides information for composing writing goals.

Chapter 4 also includes lessons to instruct students in goal writing for the Reading, Writing, Math, and Life Skills sections. In addition, students learn to write summaries for Math and Life Skills. Sample summary and goal statements are provided for student use (Atwell 1987, 117–19, 195–96). (See pp. 83, 84, 88, 90, 93, and 94.) A teacher using this book may adapt these statements to meet the needs of a particular class or situation. For example, when our students wrote the reading goals during the first quarter of the year, we did not make the entire list of reading goals available; rather, we gradually added to the list of goals throughout the year as the topics were presented in reading workshop mini-lessons. Also suggested in this section is the addition to the portfolio of a reading page photocopy from the student's current book. Students may read aloud from it during student-led parent conferences, which are discussed later in this introduction. Lesson 24 details the procedure for students to demonstrate that goals have been met. Students keep personal records of goal attainment on their goal cards, and the whole class records total goals achieved on a classroom thermometer. This way students may realize success both individually and as part of the group. The teacher plans appropriate awards for goal attainment.

Ongoing lessons are discussed in chapter 6. Ideas are presented for teachers to use during the weekly portfolio time. The students also complete a summary of the semester activities and relate these to the student exit outcomes. From our experience, students capable of using this portfolio format are also capable of understanding this important link to outcome-based education.

The end-of-the-year lessons for the portfolio are in chapter 8. Students complete a final writing sample, which is again evaluated according to the Creative Writing Checklist, and complete the writing bar graph from the beginning of the year. Year-end reading and writing surveys are used to make comparisons on the provided reflections pages. (See pp. 122, 126.) Sample strategies for reading (Smith 1985, 16, 40–41, 62–64) and writing aid students in completing their reflections. Students complete a second Math Skills Demonstration page and compare it with their original one. They also select another computer sample and another page from a reading book to photocopy. As throughout the year, students may select other pieces of work to include in their portfolios. We found that although students were aware of their progress as they attained goals during the year, their achievements were especially apparent during these end-of-the-year activities. The students understood their progress and how it was achieved, rather than seeing a grade of "C" change to a "B" without understanding why. There was a current of excitement as students compared their work samples and responses from the fall to those in the spring. We realized that, until using this portfolio format, most students had not observed their own growth over the year in such visual terms.

There is always the question of what to do with portfolios at the end of the year. It is our hope that schools committed to the portfolio format as a viable method to show student progress would develop their own systems for passing on the portfolios to the next grade. School faculties would need to decide the types of work samples that would remain in the portfolios. For example, the last writing sample of the year would stay, as would the checklist of mastered math skills. Both these items would serve as baselines for next year's teacher. Students and teacher together would then decide which other work samples would be kept and which would be removed. As part of the ongoing process from year to year, items would need to be removed as items showing higher skills replaced them.

However, when the next grade level teachers are not interested in seeing the portfolios, the portfolios go home at the end of the year as keepsakes. The increased student motivation, investment, and pride in accomplishments make the portfolio a worthwhile project even without a total school commitment.

Student-Led Parent Conference Components

In this book, we have combined our ideas for student-led parent conferences with the model presented by Little and Allan. Using the whole-child portfolio format, it is not necessary to prepare student work folders for the conferences, because the tasks of gathering work to show parents and instructing students on the relevance of their work have already been accomplished. Practicing the communication and social skills for the conference, and selecting science, social studies, and math manipulative activities for the spring conferences, are the only lessons needed.

In our model, student-led parent conferences are held three times during the school year. These three conferences are discussed in chapters 5, 7, and 9. Teachers may adjust these suggested conference times to coincide with their school's conference schedule. Additional home student-led parent conferences may be scheduled for schools without fall and spring conference times.

Chapter 5 details lessons that prepare students to use the whole-child portfolios to demonstrate their skills during fall student-led parent conferences. Provided in this chapter are the letter home to parents, a conference agenda, a rubric of expected student behaviors for conferences, parent and student evaluations, and teacher tips. This first conference familiarizes parents with the portfolio format. It also provides time for parents to give input for the Life Skills and VIP sections of the portfolio and to make comments in the Visitor Log.

In our suggested schedule, several conferences occur in the room at a given time, with the teacher circulating from group to group. There is no time allotted for a traditional, private parent-teacher conference. However, because parents may have more specific questions about class structure, academics, and behavior at the beginning of the year, the teacher may wish to schedule fall conferences with 15 to 20-minute blocks of time to speak with each parent individually. The parent and child would complete the student-led parent conference in the 30 to 45 minutes preceding or following the regular conference. This alternative schedule may meet the needs of all concerned.

It should be noted that student-led parent conferences are meant to be celebrations of student success and demonstrations of growth. This is a time for parents to express positive feelings about their student's accomplishments. It is not the time for parents to discuss serious academic or behavioral concerns with the teacher. These concerns should be dealt with as they develop through traditional parent-teacher conferences, phone calls, or notes home. However, these topics are addressed by the student in the student-led parent conference. Achievement and areas for improvement are discussed through the summaries and goals on the title pages for the different portfolio sections, and, if warranted, classroom behavior goals are written in the area of Life Skills before the conference.

Chapter 7 explains the procedures for the midyear student-led parent conferences. Students take their portfolios home to update parents on goals achieved and to gain more parental input. They also explain the semester activities that correlate to the student exit outcomes.

Student-led parent conferences for the end of the year are presented in chapter 9. The spring conferences allow parents to see their student's achievements for the entire year. Included again are a parent letter, a conference agenda, and the student and parent evaluations. In preparation for the conferences, students correlate the activities for the second semester to the student exit outcomes. They also add to the portfolios their lists of books read during the year and samples of reading journal entries from the first and the end of the year. Highlights of these conferences are the science, social studies, and math manipulative demonstrations. We did not include these activities in the fall conferences because of the time needed for students to explain the portfolio information to their parents. Students can assume these additional responsibilities in the spring because they are more familiar and confident with student-led parent conferences and the portfolio format.

Final Considerations

With the overall project now in mind, consider the following items:

1. Do you want to begin with the entire project and all sections of the portfolio, or would choosing two areas such as Writing and Life Skills be easier to manage while you are becoming familiar with this approach?

2. Are there lessons you would like to modify or omit?

3. After comparing your school calendar to the overview in the book, what modifications are necessary for the portfolio and conferences?

4. Would you benefit by asking a parent to help with the project? Suggested duties for room parents are conducting interviews for classroom jobs, assisting during portfolio mini-lessons and goal-attainment conferences, supervising coloring of the goal thermometer and stapling of individual goal squares, and organizing the decorations and refreshments for student-led parent conferences.

5. Are there other activities you would like to add to the lessons, and, if so, where would these activities be included?

6. What are the ground rules for what goes into the portfolio, what is removed, and who makes these decisions? One desirable arrangement has the teacher making some of the choices and students making others, with some guidelines being nonnegotiable. For example, the first-of-the-year writing sample may be the teacher's choice, the midyear sample may be the student's choice, and the end-of-the-year sample may be chosen together. The fact that at least three samples are collected over the year may be nonnegotiable.

7. What materials will you need to obtain from your own sources? The basic instructions and reproducibles to teach these lessons have been provided. However, the teacher needs to find more general items, such as an overhead transparency showing the proper form for a friendly letter.

8. How many items are available from your district, such as student exit outcomes, rubrics, writing guidelines, math checklists, and so on, and which of these do you want to use? Note that we do not recommend the extensive use of checklists and have not provided them unless they will be directly used to help students understand and evaluate their progress. We strongly feel that teacher time should be used for direct instruction and conferring with students rather than completing checklists.

CONCLUSION

A portfolio is an important assessment tool that is consistent with the movement in education today toward authentic tasks and outcome-based education. Because there are more intelligences than those assessed by traditional tests, the instruction and assessment of the whole child will help each student reach full potential. The whole-child portfolio takes into account all those aspects of the person that are important for life success. It also provides a vehicle to collect demonstrated performances for outcome-based education. By using the whole-child portfolio to conduct student-led parent conferences, students are given the opportunity to communicate and collaborate with their parents about their progress, reflections, and goals.

Questions About Portfolios

1. Won't portfolios take too much time away from regular instruction?

A time commitment is needed to make portfolios successful. However, the time is significantly reduced by using the information and reproducibles in this book. The step-by-step plans are easy to follow and can be modified if desired. All handouts, letters, and organizational work have been done. Teachers will note significant improvements in student responsibility and motivation. Students understand why they are doing tasks, the criteria for evaluating the tasks, and how to evaluate their own performances. We know from experience that the time is worthwhile.

2. How can I explain the portfolio concept to parents and administrators?

This book contains all the parent letters you will need for home communication. The portfolio itself, when assembled by the student, gives concise information to the reader to explain the portfolio concept and organization. This is helpful for administrators as well as for anyone who visits the portfolio.

3. My students already keep all their best work in a file. Isn't this sufficient for a portfolio?

If the desired result is simply a collection of student work, this type of file is sufficient. However, if teachers want to improve their own effectiveness and increase student responsibility, a plan is needed that involves students in setting goals and evaluating themselves. This plan should help students understand what is expected of them and what criteria will be used to evaluate them. By using the material in this book, these goals and many more can be achieved.

4. There are so many recent developments in education that I can't keep up with them. Shouldn't I wait to start portfolios until a clear direction is set by my district?

Our feeling is that it is better to be proactive than to have something given to us with a requirement for implementation.

5. What is the connection between outcome-based education and portfolios?

There is a clear connection between these two areas. Students will be demonstrating their learning rather than receiving credit for seat time. A place is needed to keep these demonstrated skills as noted in the portfolio system of the Harrison School District. (See page 6.)

6. Why do portfolios if the next grade level teachers do not even want to see them?

This is a logical question if you have not done the portfolio project outlined in this book. However, after following the guidelines presented here, we are certain you will experience the same results we did. The increased student motivation and investment, as well as the clarification of teaching goals, make it a worthwhile project even if the result at the end of the year is that the portfolio goes home as a keepsake.

7. Parents still want to see a grade and know where the student is in relation to other students. Will a portfolio do this?

This predicament is not easily resolved. Through the portfolio format, children are measured against themselves. They can see their own progress and the attainment of their own goals. Actual demonstrations of skills are collected, and the evaluations are meaningful because they are based on criteria established in the classroom. This approach to student assessment is very different from grades, which do not show what the student can actually do. Certainly, parent education is critical. Until portfolios are more widely used and accepted, it will be necessary to continue to give grades.

8. My special education students do not excel in the portfolios our school keeps for reading and writing. How can I make them feel positive about themselves?

This observation is not exclusive to the special education students. All students have strengths that cannot be recognized in a reading and writing portfolio. That is the reason we developed the whole-child portfolio. Every strength of a student needs to be valued and recognized.

9. I know very little about outcome-based education and rubrics. How can I expect my students to understand these concepts?

Using the ideas in this book, you can learn some of the basics with your students through activities that are easy to understand and apply. For in-depth study, you will need to consult your school district for current developments in outcome-based education.

10. My grade level departmentalizes in some subjects. Can this portfolio format be used when students rotate from class to class?

Definitely! The homeroom teacher would organize the portfolio at the beginning of the year, using the suggested lessons in this book. Depending on the rotations, different teachers may be responsible for the Reading, Writing, and Math sections. The science and social studies teachers could contribute to the existing sections as in our model or may choose to have separate sections in the portfolio. All teachers would also have items for the Life Skills section. Specials teachers should be encouraged to contribute to the portfolio as well. For example, the music teacher may suggest items to fit in VIP. Or an assignment in music theory could be added to the Life Skills section as an example of critical thinking.

Questions About Student-Led Parent Conferences

1. Won't there be numerous parents who still want a regular parent-teacher conference?

As stated from our research, about three parents in a classroom of 30 will prefer to also confer privately with the teacher. This book explains alternatives for scheduling student-led parent conferences to allow for this preference. (See p. 11.)

2. How can I prepare students well enough to explain their own learning?

Teachers who do not use our portfolio system have more work to prepare students. Those using our system will find that students are already knowledgeable and need only the basic preparation given in our student-led parent conference lessons.

3. Do student-led parent conferences mean more work and time for me?

Student-led parent conferences involve more true and effective collaboration between parent, students, and teachers. This collaboration does take time, but the benefits are readily apparent.

4. How do I educate parents and administrators about student-led parent conferences?

All the parent communications needed are included in this guidebook. These letters will also be helpful for informing your administrator of the concept and its benefits.

5. What are the advantages of having student-led parent conferences more than once a year?

Using our portfolio system, it is beneficial to have fall and spring student-led parent conferences because it involves parents from the beginning and makes the spring conferences much more meaningful. Parents are aware of goals early on and can help write them and reinforce them throughout the year. At the parents' request, we added a midyear student-led parent conference at home to continue parental involvement.

6. How do I reassure a student who is nervous about student-led parent conferences?

It is normal for students to be anxious with this new approach. Lesson 26 gives some tips for reassuring students. It is also normal for teachers to be anxious. By allowing sufficient time for preparation, following the guidelines in this book, and observing the students during conference rehearsals, teachers will feel more relaxed and confident about the conferences.

7. I understand that decorations and refreshments will help create a feeling of celebration, but isn't this just more work for the teacher?

A teacher has several options in this area. For example, a room parent may be recruited to handle these preparations, a student committee can take charge, or grade levels/departments may work out arrangements together to reduce the work involved.

8. How can student-led parent conferences maintain a feeling of celebration and success when I really need to let the parents know about behavioral and academic concerns?

Each student, regardless of behavior and performance, needs to have a positive time with parents to reflect on the things that are going well and where achievement is being made. Using the whole-child portfolio, you can capture the strengths of the child and value and build on those strengths. Concerns around behaviors and achievement should be addressed as they develop. Calls, notes home, and private conferences are used to handle these concerns. However, both of these areas will be addressed to some degree by the student in the student-led parent conference because achievement is discussed and areas for improvement are already understood. Behavior goals will have been written in the area of Life Skills, if needed.

9. Should brothers, sisters, and other relatives come to the conferences?

This should be decided by the teacher or the class. Our experience is that parents have communicated to other relatives how special and important this occasion is for the student leading the conference, and the extra guests have been positive additions. Memorable letters have been added to the portfolios from brothers, sisters, and other relatives at the end of the conference.

10. Will I see positive results from student-led parent conferences?

The benefits of student-led parent conferences are outlined on pages 6–7. Every teacher we have talked to about student-led parent conferences has regretted not starting this method sooner.

SUGGESTED TIMELINES

The key factors in starting a portfolio and student-led parent conference program are scheduling adequate time, planning ahead, and giving students the tools and strategies they need to assume more responsibilities. This timeline gives an overview of the time needed for each portion of the program and shows how the program is an ongoing learning and evaluation experience. Adjustments will, of course, be needed to plan around your school's calendar and conference times. In allowing adequate time, keep these points in mind:

1. Longer lessons may be divided and taught on different days.

2. Begin planning and practicing for student-led parent conferences well in advance. This increases everyone's self-confidence.

3. Maintain a minimum of one scheduled portfolio lesson per week so that goals are reviewed and continue to be of primary importance.

The following timeline is an example of a program that starts at the beginning of the school year. However, it is not necessary to wait until a new year to start this program. The second timeline gives an example for a class starting at midyear, using two sections in the portfolio.

16 / 1—Introduction

A combination of these two timelines is another option. Starting at the beginning of the year but using only two or three of the portfolio sections allows the teacher to ease into this program. Whatever timeline you create, plan ahead and create a situation that is structured for success—both for you and for the students. It may be realistic to plan two years for complete implementation of the whole-child portfolio and student-led parent conference format.

Full School Year Timeline

PAGE OR LESSON	WHEN?	WHAT TO DO?
"Advance Preparations," p. 19	Before school starts	Gather supplies and set up as outlined in "Advance Preparations."
Lessons 1, 2, 6–16	First 2 weeks (Several lessons per week)	Introduce the portfolio concept and send letter home. Students bring supplies, complete surveys, and do community-building activities.
Lessons 3–5	Third week	Students assemble the portfolio with section title pages and exit outcomes.
Lessons 17–23	Continuing through first quarter	Students organize completed work into portfolios and make VIP entries; create a portfolio rubric. Students complete first writing samples. Student and teacher write summaries and students write goals.
Lesson 24	After students have achieved some goals	Follow procedure for goal attainment.

Lessons for student-led parent conferences should begin early to build confidence and assure that students have the training needed to explain their skills and progress. These lessons may need to overlap with Lessons 17–24 during the first quarter, depending on the timing of conferences.

Lesson 25	4 weeks before fall conferences	Introduce students to conferences and send notes home.
Lessons 26, 27	3 weeks before	Introduce agenda and expectations.
Lessons 28, 29	2 weeks before	Practice for conferences.
Lessons 30, 31	1 week before	Practice and send invitations.
Lesson 32	Day after conference	Students write thank-you notes to parents.
Lesson 33	2 days after	Students evaluate conferences.
Pp. 112–113	After conferences through second quarter	Continue weekly lessons.
Refer to p. 113	End of first semester	Students complete midyear writing sample.
Lesson 34	End of first semester	Complete first semester exit outcomes.
Lesson 35	Beginning of second semester	Send the portfolios home.
Pp. 112–113	Remainder of third quarter	Continue weekly lessons.
Lessons 36–42	Fourth quarter	Students complete end-of-the-year writing sample, surveys, reflections, and students add journal entries, reading logs, and miscellaneous tasks.

Begin preparation for spring student-led parent conferences four weeks before the actual conferences. These lessons overlap with Lessons 36–42.

Lessons 43	4 weeks before conferences	Review student-led parent conferences and send notes home.
Lessons 44, 45	3 weeks before	Complete second semester exit outcomes; practice agenda.
Lessons 46, 47	2 weeks before	Students choose math, science, and social studies projects.
Lesson 48	1 week before	Continue practice.
See Lesson 32	Day after conference	Students write thank-you notes to parents.
Lesson 49	2 days after	Students evaluate conferences.
Pp. 112–113	Last 2–3 weeks	Conduct final goal-attainment conferences and have a party. Make final teacher comments. Students make final portfolio additions. Decide about portfolios for next year.

Modified Timeline

This timeline allows for a midyear start and involves the use of only three sections: Life Skills, Writing, and VIP. By choosing these, it is still possible to create a more complete whole-child portfolio rather than one that focuses just on academics. After some experience with the project, however, you will find that you will want to include all the sections of the book in order to value and assess the whole child. This timeline includes only one student-led parent conference.

PAGE OR LESSON	**WHEN?**	**WHAT TO DO?**
"Advance Preparations," p. 19	Before starting the program	Gather supplies and set up room.
Lessons 1, 2	First week	Introduce portfolio concept. Include sections on Life Skills, Writing, and VIP.
Modification	First week	Choose items from current work that can be placed in the portfolio when it is assembled.
Lessons 3–5	When students bring supplies	Students assemble the portfolios with section title pages and exit outcomes.
Modification	First month	Choose lessons from chapter 3 that fit your situation (include Lesson 15).
Lessons 18, 19	First month	Students organize work into portfolios and make VIP entries. Create a portfolio rubric.
Lesson 20	First writing sample	Students complete midyear writing sample. Use the guidelines in Lesson 20.
Modified Lessons 21–23	First month	Students and teacher write summaries. Students write goals for Writing and Life Skills only.
Lesson 24	When students have achieved some goals	Follow procedure for goal attainment.
Pp. 112–113	Third quarter	Perform ongoing lessons as appropriate.
Lesson 36	Fourth quarter	Students complete end-of-the-year writing samples.
Modified Lessons 37–38	Fourth quarter	Students complete the survey and reflections on writing.

Begin preparation for spring student-led parent conferences four weeks before the actual conferences. We recommend that you follow the guidelines for fall student-led parent conferences, beginning with Lesson 25. Teacher should use discretion in deciding how many hands-on activities the students should present. Without prior experience, most students should be able to handle one activity.

Lesson 25 Spring conferences	4 weeks before	Introduce conferences and send notes home with modifications.
Lessons 26, 27	3 weeks before	Introduce the modified agenda and expectations.
Modified Lessons 46, 47	2 weeks before	Students choose one hands-on activity.
Lessons 28, 29	2 weeks before	Practice for conferences.
Lessons 30, 31	1 week before	Practice and send invitations.
Lesson 32	Day after conference	Students write thank-you notes to parents.
Lesson 33	2 days after	Students evaluate conferences.
Pp. 112–113	Last 2–3 weeks of school	Conduct final goal-attainment conferences and have a party. Make final teacher comments. Students make final portfolio additions. Decide about portfolios for next year.

2 Getting Started

ADVANCE PREPARATIONS

Student Supply Lists

Include a three-ring notebook and five dividers with blank divider labels on student supply lists. The notebook should have a plastic cover that allows a cover page to be inserted on the front. There should be pockets on the inside front and back covers. Have students tape their names on the outside until covers and name tags are made.

If it is not possible to include these on the student supply list, or if you begin the project in the middle of the year, include these items in the first parent letter explaining the portfolio project.

Classroom Supplies

Obtain the following:

1. At least one heavy-duty three-hole punch. Develop the habit of prepunching any papers that will be inserted in the portfolios.
2. Paper hole reinforcers. Frequent use may create tears in the holes that secure papers in the notebook.
3. Self-adhesive computer labels. (See explanation on p. 74.)
4. A camera and film for taking pictures of student projects.
5. Five different colors of duplicating paper. Title pages and handouts for each section are duplicated in different colors.
6. Supplies for a sample portfolio.
7. Extra portfolio supplies. Have two volunteers place any handouts in two blank portfolios throughout the year for late enrollees.
8. A rubber stamp with your name. Use this when recording portfolio visits.

Classroom Setup

1. Clear a drawer for filing portfolio handouts and letters.
2. Designate an area for student portfolio storage. It should be visible, easily accessible, and near a table used by those visiting the portfolios. (See p. 96 for an illustration.)
3. Place two small baskets in the portfolio area. One holds blank goal-attainment pages and one holds the completed goal-attainment pages that are ready for teacher conferences.

20 / 2—Getting Started

Scheduling

Schedule about 30 minutes weekly for portfolio work. This will ensure the continuous development of the portfolio.

LESSON 1—INTRODUCING THE PORTFOLIO AND CHOOSING COVERS

Objective

Students will understand the portfolio concept. They will learn the purpose and organization of the portfolio.

Preparation

1. Prepare a sample portfolio to show the class.
2. Have cover designs and choices of colored paper ready to show students. (See pp. 21-25.) Attach a sign-up sheet to each cover design. Students sign up for their choice of cover and indicate their color preference.
3. Duplicate the parent letter (see p. 26) and the Home Responsibility Inventory (see p. 27). The color of the inventory should be the color you have chosen for the Life Skills section.

Content

1. Explain the portfolio concept to the students. Refer to the information on the portfolio cover. (See p. 21.)
2. Briefly explain the five sections of the portfolio, giving the section names and examples of what might be included in each area. A more detailed explanation is given later.
3. Show the sample cover designs. Explain that each cover must have the explanation of the portfolio concept even if students design their own covers. This explanation enables all visitors to understand the portfolio concept. Have students sign up for the designs and colors of paper for their covers. If they prefer, they may design their own covers on the blank border page that is provided. (See p. 25.)
4. Read the parent letter that will be going home and review the Home Responsibility Inventory.
5. When inventories are returned, save them for placement in the Life Skills section during Lesson 18.

Post Preparation

1. Duplicate the cover designs as indicated on the sign-up sheets.
2. Plan a brief presentation about the portfolio concept for parents during Back-to-School Night. This is also an opportunity to request the weekly help of a room parent if needed. (See p. 12 for room parent duties.)

THIS PORTFOLIO BELONGS TO

THE PORTFOLIO CONCEPT

Learning is always evolving, growing, and changing. It is never complete. Therefore, assessment must also be an ongoing process.

It is the goal of this portfolio to assess this continuous learning by capturing a rich sampling of student performance in all areas during the school year. The portfolio provides a vehicle for ongoing, collaborative reflection between the student, teacher, and parents, enabling each to become a partner in the learning process.

Rather than take time away from daily classroom work for separate assessment activities, this portfolio documents the student's performance on authentic tasks done in a meaningful context.

This portfolio contains the following:

1. A Visitor Log. We invite everyone to sign and comment when visiting the portfolio.

2. District student exit outcomes for successful living after graduation.

3. Dividers, summary sheets, and goal sheets for each of the following areas: Reading, Writing, Math, and Life Skills.

4. A VIP section for items that do not belong in other areas yet are Very Important to this Person.

From *Practical Portfolios*. ©1994. Teacher Ideas Press, P.O. Box 6633, Englewood, CO 80155-6633.

22 / 2—Getting Started

THIS PORTFOLIO BELONGS TO

_____

THE PORTFOLIO CONCEPT

Learning is always evolving, growing, and changing. It is never complete. Therefore, assessment must also be an ongoing process.

It is the goal of this portfolio to assess this continuous learning by capturing a rich sampling of student performance in all areas during the school year. The portfolio provides a vehicle for ongoing, collaborative reflection between the student, teacher, and parents, enabling each to become a partner in the learning process.

Rather than take time away from daily classroom work for separate assessment activities, this portfolio documents the student's performance on authentic tasks done in a meaningful context.

This portfolio contains the following:

1. A Visitor Log. We invite everyone to sign and comment when visiting the portfolio.

2. District student exit outcomes for successful living after graduation.

3. Dividers, summary sheets, and goal sheets for each of the following areas: Reading, Writing, Math, and Life Skills.

4. A VIP section for items that do not belong in other areas yet are Very Important to this Person.

From *Practical Portfolios*. ©1994. Teacher Ideas Press, P.O. Box 6633, Englewood, CO 80155-6633.

THIS PORTFOLIO BELONGS TO

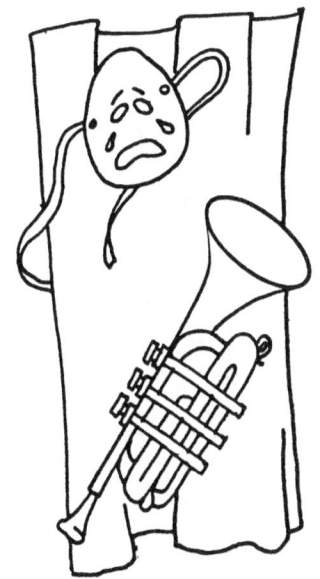

_____

THE PORTFOLIO CONCEPT

Learning is always evolving, growing, and changing. It is never complete. Therefore, assessment must also be an ongoing process.

It is the goal of this portfolio to assess this continuous learning by capturing a rich sampling of student performance in all areas during the school year. The portfolio provides a vehicle for ongoing, collaborative reflection between the student, teacher, and parents, enabling each to become a partner in the learning process.

Rather than take time away from daily classroom work for separate assessment activities, this portfolio documents the student's performance on authentic tasks done in a meaningful context.

This portfolio contains the following:

1. A Visitor Log. We invite everyone to sign and comment when visiting the portfolio.

2. District student exit outcomes for successful living after graduation.

3. Dividers, summary sheets, and goal sheets for each of the following areas: Reading, Writing, Math, and Life Skills.

4. A VIP section for items that do not belong in other areas yet are Very Important to this Person.

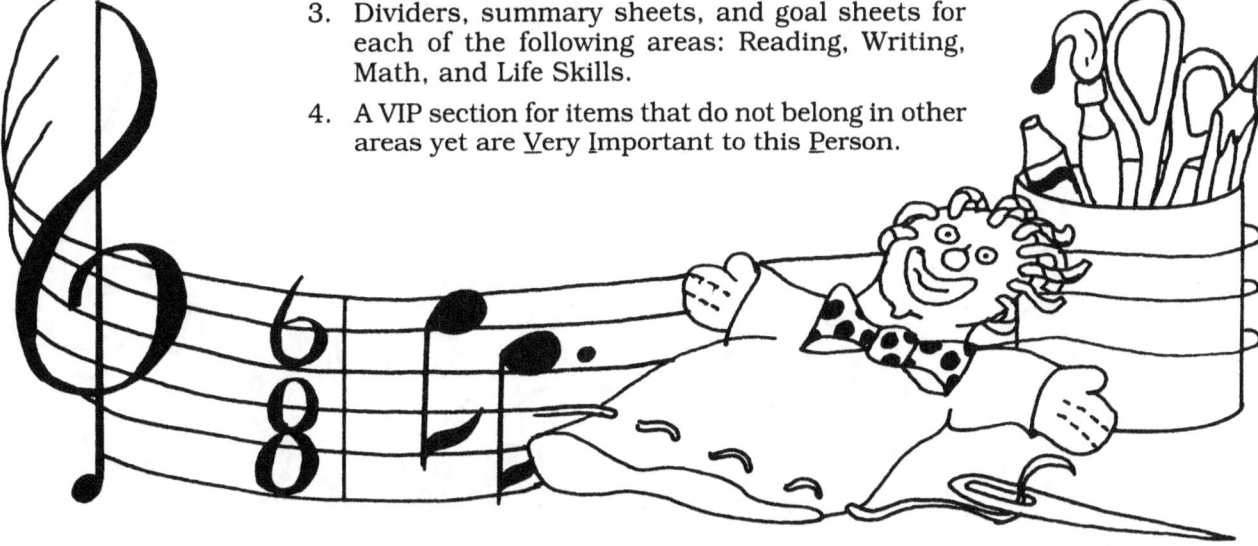

From *Practical Portfolios*. ©1994. Teacher Ideas Press, P.O. Box 6633, Englewood, CO 80155-6633.

THIS PORTFOLIO BELONGS TO

_____

THE PORTFOLIO CONCEPT

Learning is always evolving, growing, and changing. It is never complete. Therefore, assessment must also be an ongoing process.

It is the goal of this portfolio to assess this continuous learning by capturing a rich sampling of student performance in all areas during the school year. The portfolio provides a vehicle for ongoing, collaborative reflection between the student, teacher, and parents, enabling each to become a partner in the learning process.

Rather than take time away from daily classroom work for separate assessment activities, this portfolio documents the student's performance on authentic tasks done in a meaningful context.

This portfolio contains the following:

1. A Visitor Log. We invite everyone to sign and comment when visiting the portfolio.

2. District student exit outcomes for successful living after graduation.

3. Dividers, summary sheets, and goal sheets for each of the following areas: Reading, Writing, Math, and Life Skills.

4. A VIP section for items that do not belong in other areas yet are Very Important to this Person.

From *Practical Portfolios*. ©1994. Teacher Ideas Press, P.O. Box 6633, Englewood, CO 80155-6633.

THIS PORTFOLIO BELONGS TO

THE PORTFOLIO CONCEPT

Learning is always evolving, growing, and changing. It is never complete. Therefore, assessment must also be an ongoing process.

It is the goal of this portfolio to assess this continuous learning by capturing a rich sampling of student performance in all areas during the school year. The portfolio provides a vehicle for ongoing, collaborative reflection between the student, teacher, and parents, enabling each to become a partner in the learning process.

Rather than take time away from daily classroom work for separate assessment activities, this portfolio documents the student's performance on authentic tasks done in a meaningful context.

This portfolio contains the following:

1. A Visitor Log. We invite everyone to sign and comment when visiting the portfolio.

2. District student exit outcomes for successful living after graduation.

3. Dividers, summary sheets, and goal sheets for each of the following areas: Reading, Writing, Math, and Life Skills.

4. A VIP section for items that do not belong in other areas yet are Very Important to this Person.

Date_____

Dear Parents,

    This year your student will be participating in a very exciting program through the use of the student portfolio. The portfolio is a collection of selected writing pieces, projects, inventories, and assignments from the year that will be used for ongoing assessment. The use of the portfolio will enable students to develop responsibility for their own learning. They will learn to evaluate their own work and to set realistic goals.

    You, as parents, will have an important role also. I will need your help completing inventories, evaluating your student's work, and writing comments in the portfolio. Complete details of the portfolio will be presented at Back-to-School Night on _____.

    In addition, this year we will have student-led parent conferences at the end of the first quarter and again during the last quarter of the year. Each student will use the portfolio to demonstrate achievement in the areas of reading, writing, math, and life skills. The student is in charge of conducting the student-led parent conference. Research has shown that this format increases student ownership, accountability, and pride. Each parent will also have the opportunity to speak with the teacher in a traditional parent-teacher conference if desired. The portfolio will also be sent home for a midyear conference at the beginning of second semester.

    I hope you will be as excited about the student portfolio as I am. Please complete and return the attached inventory that will be included in the Life Skills section of the portfolio. You may send it to school or bring it to Back-to-School Night. I look forward to seeing you.

Sincerely,

From *Practical Portfolios*. ©1994. Teacher Ideas Press, P.O. Box 6633, Englewood, CO 80155-6633.

Student Name_____

Date_____

HOME RESPONSIBILITY INVENTORY

Dear Parents,

    Many of the life skills that students acquire are developed in the home. Students who demonstrate responsibility and initiative at home will often demonstrate these at school and in other areas of their lives. By including a record of home accomplishments in the portfolio, these efforts can be recognized and rewarded at school. The purpose is not to judge or evaluate where the child is currently. Rather, this will record the student's current accomplishments, whatever they may be, in order to set goals for future growth. Please take a few moments to complete the form below. This will be done again in the spring. Thank you!

1. My child is responsible for performing the following chores on a weekly/daily basis:

    My child usually does the items mentioned above without being told.
        yes   sometimes   no

2. My child is responsible for helping with the following as needed:

    My child usually does the items mentioned above without being told.
        yes   sometimes   no

3. My child shows responsibility and initiative in completing homework.
        yes   sometimes   no

4. My child independently manages some amount of money on a routine basis.
        always   occasionally   never

5. I feel the amount of reading done by my child at home, either with a parent or independently,
       is about right   needs to increase some   needs to increase a lot

PARENT SIGNATURE _____

From *Practical Portfolios.* ©1994. Teacher Ideas Press, P.O. Box 6633, Englewood, CO 80155-6633.

28 / 2—Getting Started

LESSON 2—DECORATING COVERS

Objective

Students will decorate portfolio covers and make name tags.

Preparation

1. Have available the duplicated covers from the postpreparation in Lesson 1.
2. Cut tagboard strips for the outer bindings of the notebooks. The strips should be about 1 x 6 inches. Use stiff paper such as tagboard to make it easier to insert the name tag into the binding.

Content

1. Distribute covers. Have students color the borders and large printed letters. The block of type labeled "The Portfolio Concept" should not be colored.
2. Have students write their names on the tagboard strips.
3. Have students insert the covers and the name tags. (See illustration above.)

LESSON 3—ASSEMBLING THE PORTFOLIOS

Objective

Students will label dividers, insert title pages, and place Visitor Logs in their portfolios. Students will have a general understanding of the contents of each section.

Preparation

Duplicate the Visitor Log and title pages in colors designated for each section. Duplicate the "continued" page in all five colors. (See pp. 29-35.)

Content

1. Label dividers in the following order: Life Skills, Reading, Writing, Math, and VIP.
2. Insert the section title pages and the "continued" pages behind the appropriate dividers. Because these pages will receive the most use, it is beneficial to apply paper hole reinforcers in advance.
3. After reviewing the explanation at the top of the Visitor Log, place it in the front pocket.
4. Explain the contents of each section as written on the title pages and give examples of items to be included.

VISITOR LOG

It is very important that all visitors, including the student, record their visits to the portfolio. This allows a running record of how often and for what purpose the portfolio is used. The work involved in creating and maintaining this portfolio will be well justified by frequent visits from many people, including teachers, students, parents, and administrators.

DATE	NAME	PURPOSE	VISITOR COMMENTS

From *Practical Portfolios*. ©1994. Teacher Ideas Press, P.O. Box 6633, Englewood, CO 80155-6633.

LIFE SKILLS

Life skills include all the skills the student will need to be successful in life. Reading, writing, and math are part of these life skills. However, each of these academic areas has a separate section in this portfolio. Suggested items to include are:

Self-evaluation/monitoring records
Learning style information
Computer skills samples
Cooperative group skills
Career awareness program records
Sample application and interview records
Peer tutor and other job evaluations
Home inventories showing home responsibilities and skills of the student
Self-awareness data (interest inventories, sharing, and autobiography)

Critical thinking skills
Health and social issues
Cultural studies
Positive self-talk
Job shadow records

The area below is provided for periodic synthesis and summarization of portfolio data in order to look at past and future goals. Synthesis is a critical component of portfolio assessment. It should be done on a regular basis and should include the student.

DATE	SUMMARY	DATE	GOALS	DATE ATTAINED

From *Practical Portfolios.* ©1994. Teacher Ideas Press, P.O. Box 6633, Englewood, CO 80155-6633.

Lesson 3—Assembling the Portfolios / 31

READING

This section gives an overview of student abilities in all areas of the reading process. Suggested items to include are

Reading surveys completed by the student
An ongoing list of books and genres read by the student
Photocopies of different reading book pages
Sample reading journal entries (literature response)
Teacher anecdotal records
Notes of conferences between teacher and student
Any checklists used in reading
Reflections on the year's achievements and activities in reading

The area below is provided for periodic synthesis and summarization of portfolio data in order to look at past and future goals. Synthesis is a critical component of portfolio assessment. It should be done on a regular basis and should include the student.

DATE	SUMMARY	DATE	GOALS	DATE ATTAINED

From *Practical Portfolios*. ©1994. Teacher Ideas Press, P.O. Box 6633, Englewood, CO 80155-6633.

WRITING

This section includes many types of writing and may include pieces in various stages of the writing process. Suggested items to include are

Writing surveys completed by the student
Drafts and final copies of expository, creative, and persuasive writing
Social studies and science reports
Research papers
Anecdotal records and conference records
Handwriting and spelling work
Reflections on the year's achievements and activities in writing
Functional writing such as checks, applications, letters, invitations, lists, picture captions, articles, and so on
District checklist of writing skills

The area below is provided for periodic synthesis and summarization of portfolio data in order to look at past and future goals. Synthesis is a critical component of portfolio assessment. It should be done on a regular basis and should include the student.

DATE	SUMMARY	DATE	GOALS	DATE ATTAINED

From *Practical Portfolios*. ©1994. Teacher Ideas Press, P.O. Box 6633, Englewood, CO 80155-6633.

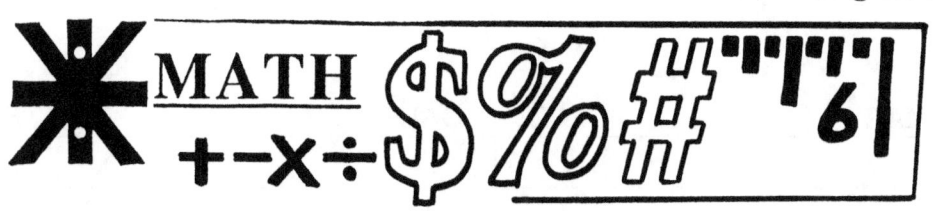

This section gives an overview of student understanding of math concepts. Suggested items to include are

Functional math records
Strategies used successfully by student for problem solving
Sample math journal entries
Classroom work, projects
Student's personal graph for math facts progress
District checklist of math skills
Math Skills Demonstration pages

The area below is provided for periodic synthesis and summarization of portfolio data in order to look at past and future goals. Synthesis is a critical component of portfolio assessment. It should be done on a regular basis and should include the student.

DATE	SUMMARY	DATE	GOALS	DATE ATTAINED

From *Practical Portfolios*. ©1994. Teacher Ideas Press, P.O. Box 6633, Englewood, CO 80155-6633.

Continued

DATE	SUMMARY	DATE	GOALS	DATE ATTAINED

V.I.P.

Each student may want to include items in the portfolio that do not fit in the preceding sections. This section announces the activities and events to be celebrated that are Very Important to this Person.

Examples of VIP entries are sports, music, art, contests, trips, or anything not included elsewhere in the portfolio.

STUDENT COMMENTS	VISITOR COMMENTS

From *Practical Portfolios*. ©1994. Teacher Ideas Press, P.O. Box 6633, Englewood, CO 80155-6633.

LESSON 4—STUDENT EXIT OUTCOMES

Objective

Students will understand district exit outcomes for high school graduates and the relationship of the exit outcomes to current classroom instruction.

Preparation

1. Prepare and duplicate a handout of your district's exit outcomes. If these are not yet available in your district, you may use the outcomes provided. Most districts have similar outcomes. Use a color other than the colors selected for the five portfolio sections, if possible. The example Student Exit Outcomes page includes a blank area in each box for use in Lesson 5. (See p. 37.) Students illustrate the meaning of each outcome. The visual representations help students explain the exit outcomes during student-led parent conferences. You may want to include similar blank spaces on your handout if you are using your own district's outcomes.
2. Prepare an overhead transparency of your handout.
3. Prepare several examples of the relationships between the outcomes and current activities to share with your students. (See Content, step 2 below, for examples.)
4. Gather poster-making materials. You may want to have the outcomes already printed on the posters in large letters to assure that they can be seen. Students design the artwork and color in the letters.

Content

1. Distribute the Student Exit Outcomes page and display the overhead transparency. Explain the exit outcomes for your school district, using examples to clarify the meaning of each one. Explain that all students are expected to work toward these outcomes by meeting established criteria throughout their school years. For example, the criteria for the effective communicator outcome at sixth grade might be the demonstration of a paragraph written to given specifications. Regardless of whether the criteria have been defined for your district, it is important that students of all ages understand the final outcomes and that all the current activities and assignments are designed to help them meet these outcomes.
2. Show relationships between these exit outcomes and several activities the class has completed or will complete this year. For example, self-monitoring (see Lesson 9, p. 50) is directly related to the outcome "Self-Directed Learner." Drawing a conclusion from a science experiment involves the outcome "Complex Thinker."
3. Give two more class activities and ask students to name the appropriate outcomes.
4. Students place the Student Exit Outcomes page in their portfolios in front of the Life Skills divider.
5. Assign groups for making posters. Each group makes a poster for one exit outcome. Due to the illustration size, the picture of the classroom on page 96 does not show illustrations on the posters. However, sample illustrations done by students are on page 39.
6. Give directions for making posters. Posters need large lettering and pictures.
7. Display the completed posters in the room. Refer to them often when doing lessons or activities to show their relationships to the exit outcomes.

JEFFERSON COUNTY PUBLIC SCHOOLS, COLORADO
STUDENT EXIT OUTCOMES

The roles expected of the successful adult in the twenty-first century

EFFECTIVE COMMUNICATOR Expresses ideas using a wide variety of methods including written and spoken languages, math, and the arts.	QUALITY WORKER Creates high-quality products, services, and performances through both independent actions and teamwork.
SELF-DIRECTED LEARNER Takes responsibility for self-improvement and ongoing learning. Plans, evaluates, and adapts, using the lessons of the past and forecasts of the future.	COMPLEX THINKER Analyzes, evaluates, and synthesizes information and ideas from multiple resources to make responsible, informed decisions. Applies flexible and creative ideas to identify and solve problems.
ETHICAL PERSON Uses a strong sense of one's own identity and personal values to make responsible decisions that balance self-interest with the interests of others. Displays qualities that the community values, including caring and respect for others, honesty, integrity, loyalty, and fairness.	RESPONSIBLE CITIZEN Develops an awareness and an understanding of one's own cultural and ethnic heritage as well as that of others. Promotes and supports attitudes, practices, and policies that enhance the quality of life in our multi-cultural, interdependent world.

THE FOUNDATION—Outcomes are built on a foundation of

<u>Basic Skills</u> Includes reading, writing, listening, speaking, and mathematics
<u>Cultural Knowledge</u> As learned from the social studies, the sciences, literature, and the arts
<u>Personal Well-being</u> Characterized by physical and mental health

Credit to Jefferson County Public Schools

From *Practical Portfolios*. ©1994. Teacher Ideas Press, P.O. Box 6633, Englewood, CO 80155-6633.

38 / 2—Getting Started

LESSON 5—STUDENT ILLUSTRATIONS OF EXIT OUTCOMES

Objective

Students will review the exit outcomes and illustrate each one.

Note: This activity can be completed anytime before the first student-led parent conferences. Use it immediately to help students gain a better understanding of the exit outcomes, or use it later as a review and reinforcement of the information you covered in Lesson 4.

Preparation

1. Prepare examples to help students brainstorm ideas for illustrations.
2. Students already have personal copies of the Student Exit Outcomes page in their portfolios.

Content

1. Have students turn to the Student Exit Outcomes page in their portfolios.
2. Review and discuss the meaning of each exit outcome. Refer to the posters on the wall and the illustrations for each one.
3. Brainstorm other ideas for illustrating each outcome.
4. Allow student work time. Have students sketch illustrations in pencil and then color the illustrations when satisfied with the artwork. (See p. 39 for examples.)

Lesson 4—Student Exit Outcomes / 39

JEFFERSON COUNTY PUBLIC SCHOOLS, COLORADO
STUDENT EXIT OUTCOMES

The roles expected of the successful adult in the twenty-first century

EFFECTIVE COMMUNICATOR Expresses ideas using a wide variety of methods including written and spoken languages, math, and the arts.  	QUALITY WORKER Creates high-quality products, services, and performances through both independent actions and teamwork.  Work hard! Do it right!
SELF-DIRECTED LEARNER Takes responsibility for self-improvement and ongoing learning. Plans, evaluates, and adapts, using the lessons of the past and forecasts of the future. I can do it! 	COMPLEX THINKER Analyzes, evaluates, and synthesizes information and ideas from multiple resources to make responsible, informed decisions. Applies flexible and creative ideas to identify and solve problems.  Use all my brain power!
ETHICAL PERSON Uses a strong sense of one's own identity and personal values to make responsible decisions that balance self-interest with the interests of others. Displays qualities that the community values, including caring and respect for others, honesty, integrity, loyalty, and fairness.  Decision? 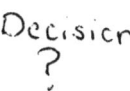	RESPONSIBLE CITIZEN Develops an awareness and an understanding of one's own cultural and ethnic heritage as well as that of others. Promotes and supports attitudes, practices, and policies that enhance the quality of life in our multicultural, interdependent world.

THE FOUNDATION—Outcomes are built on a foundation of

Basic Skills Includes reading, writing, listening, speaking, and mathematics
Cultural Knowledge As learned from the social studies, the sciences, literature, and the arts
Personal Well-being Characterized by physical and mental health

Credit to Jefferson County Public Schools

From *Practical Portfolios*. ©1994. Teacher Ideas Press, P.O. Box 6633, Englewood, CO 80155-6633.

3 Suggested First-of-the-Year Portfolio Lessons

LESSON 6—WRITING AN AUTOBIOGRAPHICAL LETTER

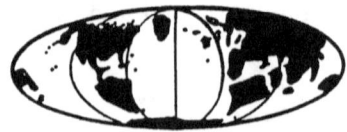

Objective

Students will review the friendly letter format. They will summarize information about themselves as an introduction to the teacher and the other students.

Preparation

1. Prepare an overhead transparency of a friendly letter.
2. For sharing purposes, write an autobiographical letter.

Content

1. Review the friendly letter format with students, using an overhead transparency.
2. Brainstorm types of information that students may want to include in their letters, such as family, pets, sports, hobbies, favorite school subjects, travel, and so on.
3. Have students write letters about themselves.
4. Have students proofread their letters and make corrections.
5. Collect all the letters. When time allows, read each letter aloud without disclosing the name of the writer. Include your own letter. Have students guess who wrote each letter.
6. Save letters to place in the Life Skills section during Lesson 18.

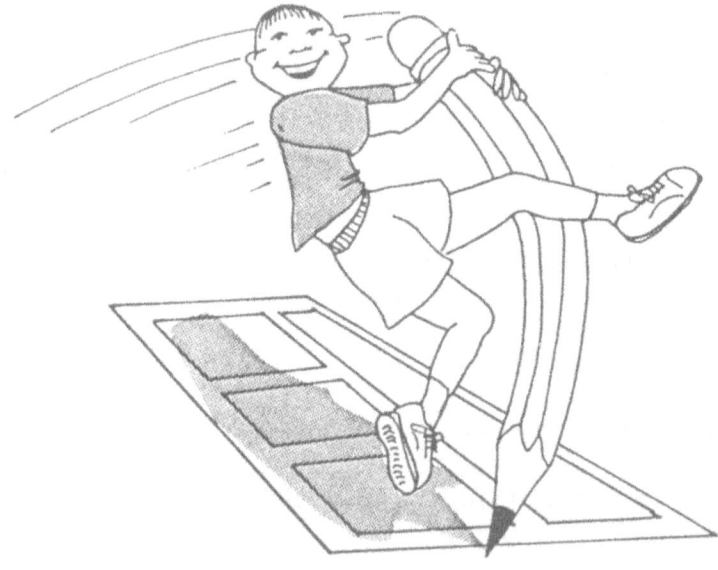

LESSON 7—COOPERATIVE LEARNING

Objective

Students will understand the concept of cooperative learning, how it will be used in the classroom, and how it relates to real life.

Preparation

1. Duplicate Cooperative Learning page (see p. 42) on the color of paper that has been designated for Life Skills.
2. Prepare an example of the cooperative learning activity. Make an overhead transparency of the example, if desired.

Content

1. Discuss cooperative learning. Cooperative learning is working together with members of a group on an assigned task and involves the skills of listening, speaking, taking turns, compromising, and encouraging.
2. Explain that these skills will be emphasized in group tasks throughout the year.
3. Give examples of how cooperative skills apply to real-life situations, such as working cooperatively with team members on the job.
4. Distribute the Cooperative Learning page.
5. Share the example done in Preparation.
6. Have students write a paragraph on the skills they will use to work cooperatively in groups throughout the year. You may want students to prepare a rough draft, proofread, and then copy the paragraph on the page provided. Allow student work time.
7. Share completed assignments as a class. Collect the assignments.
8. Save this activity for inclusion in the Life Skills section during Lesson 18.

42 / 3—Suggested First-of-the-Year Portfolio Lessons

Name: _____
Date: _____

Write a paragraph that describes what you will do this year to work cooperatively in a group.

Cooperative Learning

From *Practical Portfolios*. ©1994. Teacher Ideas Press, P.O. Box 6633, Englewood, CO 80155-6633.

LESSON 8—CREATING A CLASSROOM RUBRIC FOR BEHAVIOR EXPECTATIONS

Objective

Students will understand the term "rubric" and how a rubric is used. Students will create a rubric for classroom behavior expectations.

Preparation

1. Make a transparency of a sample rubric. (See pp. 44–49.)
2. Obtain posterboard.

Content

1. Define rubric. A rubric is a description of what a learner will do in order to meet the required standard. These descriptions are organized into four categories: "Novice" is severely below the standard, "emerging" is slightly below the standard, "standard" is the expected behavior for proficiency, and "exceeds standard" goes beyond the standard. (See chapter 1, p. 13, for more information on rubrics and outcome-based education.)
2. Present an example of a rubric.
3. Explain that the class will create a rubric for classroom behavior expectations to be used for the year.
4. Brainstorm the student behaviors that contribute to a good learning environment. (See example on p. 44.)
5. List these behaviors as the standard.
6. Develop the "novice," "emerging," and "exceeds standard" categories.

Post Preparation

Record the rubric on large posterboard for classroom display.

Rubric for Behavior Expectations

EXCEEDS STANDARD **EX**	I use all behaviors in the standard. I help other students when requested by the teacher. I complete activities or assignments and do extra credit or enrichment. I show appropriate leadership by encouraging other students to achieve standard behaviors.
STANDARD **ST**	I demonstrate appropriate body language when lessons are presented (eye contact, quiet mouth and body). I begin the activity or assignment as soon as the directions are completed by the teacher. I complete assignments on time. I use my time wisely if I am finished with an assignment. I understand directions, or I ask questions when I don't understand I work cooperatively in groups by using cooperative group skills. I remain seated unless it is appropriate to be out of my seat. I respect myself and the rights of others. I have my materials daily, and I am punctual.
EMERGING **EM**	I demonstrate appropriate body language some of the time. I need reminders to begin the activity or assignment. I have some incomplete or late assignments. Sometimes I don't ask for help when I don't understand directions. Sometimes I don't work cooperatively in groups. Sometimes I am out of my seat when I shouldn't be. Sometimes I give put-downs to myself and others. I ask to borrow materials because I forget to bring mine. I am tardy, but I am generally in school each day.
NOVICE **NO**	I do not demonstrate appropriate body language. I do not begin the activity or assignment even with reminders. I do not complete my assignments on time. I don't ask for help when I don't understand directions. I need to be removed from cooperative group activities. I am frequently out of my seat when I shouldn't be. I give put-downs to myself and others. I don't have materials so I sit doing nothing. I am often absent or tardy.

Rubric for Silent Reading

EXCEEDS STANDARD
EX
- I keep my eyes on my book, reading for a half hour, and could easily read longer.
- I ignore distractions and don't talk to or notice others; I sit in one spot.
- I am eager to finish books and start new ones.
- I always bring my book to class; I look for new ones to read.
- I read much more than 100 pages per week, finding extra time to read.
- I comprehend what I read, can easily explain it to others, and extend my reading to other areas.

STANDARD
ST
- I keep my eyes on my book and read for a half hour.
- I ignore distractions and don't talk to or notice others; I sit in one spot.
- I finish the book I start.
- I bring my book to class.
- I read about 100 pages per week (combined reading in school and at home).
- I comprehend what I read; I can summarize it and explain it to others.

EMERGING
EM
- I read for a half hour but occasionally look around.
- I am bothered by distractions and sometimes talk, move, or fidget.
- I lose my place in my book and have to start over.
- I sometimes forget to bring my book to class.
- I read less than 100 pages per week.
- I sometimes have trouble summarizing what I read and explaining it to others.

NOVICE
NO
- I can't read for a half hour; I look around or pretend to read.
- I am interested in distractions and cause them by talking, moving, or fidgeting.
- I lose my place and forget what I read.
- I frequently forget my book.
- I have trouble completing books.
- I am confused about what I read and can't explain it to others.

Credit to Kathy Vandamme, Jefferson County, Colorado.

Rubric for Reading Discussion

EXCEEDS STANDARD EX	I listen to others, state worthwhile comments and questions, and encourage openness and understanding. I predict, analyze, compare and contrast, and find patterns in major story elements, including setting, characters, plot (problem, climax, solution), main idea, mood, voice, and author's style. I creatively apply the discussion to other situations apart from the book. I clearly share my thoughts and opinions with others orally and in written responses. I express and explain my feelings about my book.
STANDARD ST	I listen to others and state worthwhile comments and questions. I predict, analyze, compare and contrast, and find patterns in major story elements, including setting, characters, plot (problem, climax, solution), main idea, mood, voice, and author's style. I share my thoughts and opinions with others orally and in written responses. I express my feelings about my book.
EMERGING EM	I am occasionally distracted and bored, or I fidget, when listening to others. I sometimes can predict, analyze, compare and contrast, and find patterns in major story elements, including setting, characters, plot (problem, climax, solution), main idea, mood, voice, and author's style. I describe my thoughts and opinions only generally in my oral or written responses. I express my feelings only sometimes about my book.
NOVICE NO	I don't listen to others. I can't predict, analyze, compare and contrast, and find patterns in major story elements, including setting, characters, plot (problem, climax, solution), main idea, mood, voice, and author's style. I do not describe my thoughts and opinions with others orally or in written responses. I do not explain my feelings about my book.

Credit to Kathy Vandamme, Jefferson County, Colorado.

Rubric for Silent Writing

EXCEEDS STANDARD
EX
- I write for a half hour and could easily write longer.
- I ignore distractions and don't talk to or notice others; I sit in one spot.
- I brainstorm ideas, then write; the words flow easily.
- I am eager to make changes in wording to help my writing become stronger and clearer.
- I use strong, complete sentences and organize my writing by paragraphs.
- Spelling and punctuation are extremely good; my final copy is very neat.
- I communicate clearly and effectively; my writing is interesting and understandable.

STANDARD
ST
- I keep focused and write for a half hour.
- I ignore distractions and don't talk to or notice others; I sit in one spot.
- I brainstorm ideas, then write, choosing to get words down quickly rather than judge them.
- I read my writing thoughtfully, looking for places that are weak; then I write my paper again making many changes.
- I use complete sentences and am beginning to organize my writing by paragraphs.
- I correct spelling and punctuation; my final copy is neat and clean.
- I communicate clearly; my writing is understandable.

EMERGING
EM
- I write for a half hour but occasionally have to stop and regain my concentration.
- I am bothered by distractions and sometimes talk, move, or fidget.
- I forget to brainstorm and just write; sometimes it is hard to get words down.
- I don't really like to rewrite parts; I usually change only a few words.
- My sentences are sometimes weak; I do not use paragraphs.
- I correct some spelling and punctuation, but there are still mistakes; my final copy could look better.
- My writing is somewhat unclear; it is hard to follow, confusing, or boring.
- I look around and pretend to write; I can't write for a half hour.
- I am interested in distractions and cause them by talking, moving, or fidgeting.

NOVICE
NO
- I don't brainstorm and I write very slowly.
- I write my piece once; I do not change the wording.
- My sentences are weak; I do not use paragraphs.
- I do not fix spelling or punctuation. There are many errors, and my final copy is messy.
- My writing does not make sense to others; it does not communicate effectively.

Credit to Kathy Vandamme, Jefferson County, Colorado.

Rubric for Writing Discussion

EXCEEDS STANDARD **EX**	I listen to others, make specific and helpful comments, and encourage openness and understanding. I willingly share my writing and clearly explain my thoughts and feelings. I judge suggestions against my own needs and standards, applying those that I find most helpful.
STANDARD **ST**	I listen to others and make helpful comments. I share my writing and explain my thoughts and feelings. I judge suggestions against my own needs and standards, applying those that I find most helpful.
EMERGING **EM**	I am occasionally distracted and bored, or I fidget, when listening to others. I sometimes share my writing; I explain my thoughts and feelings in a general way. I have trouble identifying my own needs and applying suggestions.
NOVICE **NO**	I don't listen to others. I don't like to share my writing and have trouble explaining my thoughts and feelings. I am unaware of my needs and standards and don't apply suggestions.

Credit to Kathy Vandamme, Jefferson County, Colorado.

Rubric for Biography Report

EXCEEDS STANDARD EX	I fully explain the four main sections in my report: birth, early life, adult life, and major accomplishments. I write creative introductory and concluding paragraphs in my report. I write in complete sentences and in paragraph form. I have a creative cover for my report. I use more than three sources in writing my report. I write my bibliography in correct form. I include extra artwork, diagrams, models, dioramas, or other displays with my report.
STANDARD ST	I include four main sections in my report: birth, early life, adult life, and major accomplishments. I write interesting introductory and concluding paragraphs in my report. I write in complete sentences and in paragraph form. My cover has decorative letters and a colorful design or picture. I use three sources in writing my report. I write my bibliography in correct form.
EMERGING EM	I include four main sections in my report: birth, early life, adult life, and major accomplishments. However, my information is incomplete. I don't have introductory or concluding paragraphs in my report. I use complete sentences inconsistently; I indent only some of my paragraphs correctly. I write only the title on my cover; I do not use any artwork. I use only two sources in writing my report. I don't follow the correct form in writing my bibliography.
NOVICE NO	I have fewer than four main sections in my report. I don't have introductory or concluding paragraphs in my report. I write my report with incomplete sentences and in one paragraph. I don't have a cover for my report. I use only one source in writing my report; I don't have a bibliography.

LESSON 9—SELF-MONITORING

Objective

Students will understand the concept of self-monitoring and demonstrate the ability to monitor themselves.

Note: Plan to do this lesson several days after creating the rubric for behavior expectations. (See p. 44.) Do this activity during another lesson such as science or social studies. Complete steps 1 and 2 of Content to introduce the concept; then begin your curriculum lesson.

Preparation

1. Duplicate the Self-Monitoring page in the Life Skills color and cut it in half. (See p. 52.)
2. Decide on a time to do the activity. This may be done intermittently throughout the day or several times during one lesson.

Content

1. Explain the concept of self-monitoring, how it is used, and why. Self-monitoring is a tool to help students become more aware of their behavior and work habits. Students can use this information to help them set goals, monitor their progress, and demonstrate proof of goal attainment. This strategy helps create student ownership in identifying areas for improvement, setting realistic goals, and monitoring progress. Self-monitoring is a critical skill in the world of work because employers expect workers to monitor and evaluate themselves.
2. Distribute Self-Monitoring pages. Have students write their names, the date, and the behavior or expectation that they are monitoring. This particular lesson is monitoring behavior according to the Rubric for Behavior Expectations.
3. Continue with a lesson such as science or social studies.
4. Five minutes into the lesson, stop and ask students to think for a moment about their behavior. Have them circle the letters on the Self-Monitoring page that correspond to the letter on the behavior rubric that describes their behavior. If they have some characteristics in one and some in another, they should place a mark between two categories. If desired, the time of day can be recorded on the line above each column.
5. Return to the science or social studies lesson. Repeat step 4 at one or two other intervals or continue with self-monitoring of behavior throughout the day.
6. Place a completed Self-Monitoring page from the beginning of the year in the Life Skills section of the portfolio during Lesson 18. (See the completed sample of a Self-Monitoring page on p. 51.)

Other Uses for Self-Monitoring

Monitoring on-task behavior or amount of work completed
Adherence to cooperative group guidelines
Following reading and writing workshop rubrics
Class discussion participation

Note: A rubric is not needed for each item that students monitor for themselves. For example, explain the standard you are expecting for class discussion and have the students rate themselves accordingly.

Lesson 9—Self-Monitoring / 51

Name __Jane__   Date __9/11__   Self-Monitoring for __Behavior Rubric__

| 9:00 | 9:20 | 10:15 | 11:00 | 12:00 |
| EX | EX | EX | EX | EX |

| ST | ST | ST | ST | (ST) |

| | Em+ | | Em+ | |
| (EM) | EM | EM | EM | EM |

| NO | NO | (NO) | NO | NO |

Name_____ Date_____ Self-Monitoring for _____

EX	EX	EX	EX	EX
ST	ST	ST	ST	ST
EM	EM	EM	EM	EM
NO	NO	NO	NO	NO

- -

Name_____ Date_____ Self-Monitoring for _____

EX	EX	EX	EX	EX
ST	ST	ST	ST	ST
EM	EM	EM	EM	EM
NO	NO	NO	NO	NO

From *Practical Portfolios*. ©1994. Teacher Ideas Press, P.O. Box 6633, Englewood, CO 80155-6633.

LESSON 10—SHARING PAGE

Objective

Students will increase awareness of self and others.

Preparation

1. Choose one of the Sharing pages or create your own. (See examples on pp. 54–56.) It is helpful to start with a nonpersonal topic such as a trip or a vacation.
2. Complete the teacher portion of the Sharing page before duplicating.
3. Duplicate the Sharing page in the color designated for Life Skills.

Content

1. Explain that the more people know about themselves and others, the easier it is to get along and be more productive. This activity can also build self-esteem and a sense of community in your classroom.
2. Explain that the Sharing page is designed for students to a) become aware of teacher self-reflections, b) do student self-reflections, c) share self-reflections, and d) hear the self-reflections of others.
3. Introduce the topic of the Sharing page. The topics may be those included on the following worksheets or may be opinions, memories, favorite activities, and so on. Share your response. Ask students to record their responses in the self section.
4. Instruct students to share their responses with a partner. Have students record their partner's response in the partner area.
5. Discuss what students learned from the activity. For example, students may find they have things in common with another student or may discover someone who has an interesting background or hobby.
6. Collect and save Sharing pages for Lesson 18.

Other Topics for Sharing Pages

If I had one wish, I'd wish ...
I would like to try to ...
My feelings are hurt when ...
Three things I really don't like are ...
My most embarrassing moment was when ...
The best present I ever received was ...
My favorite subject in school is ...
I get nervous when I ...

54 / 3—Suggested First-of-the-Year Portfolio Lessons

SHARING PAGE

Name _____ Date _____

One of the best trips I've ever taken was …

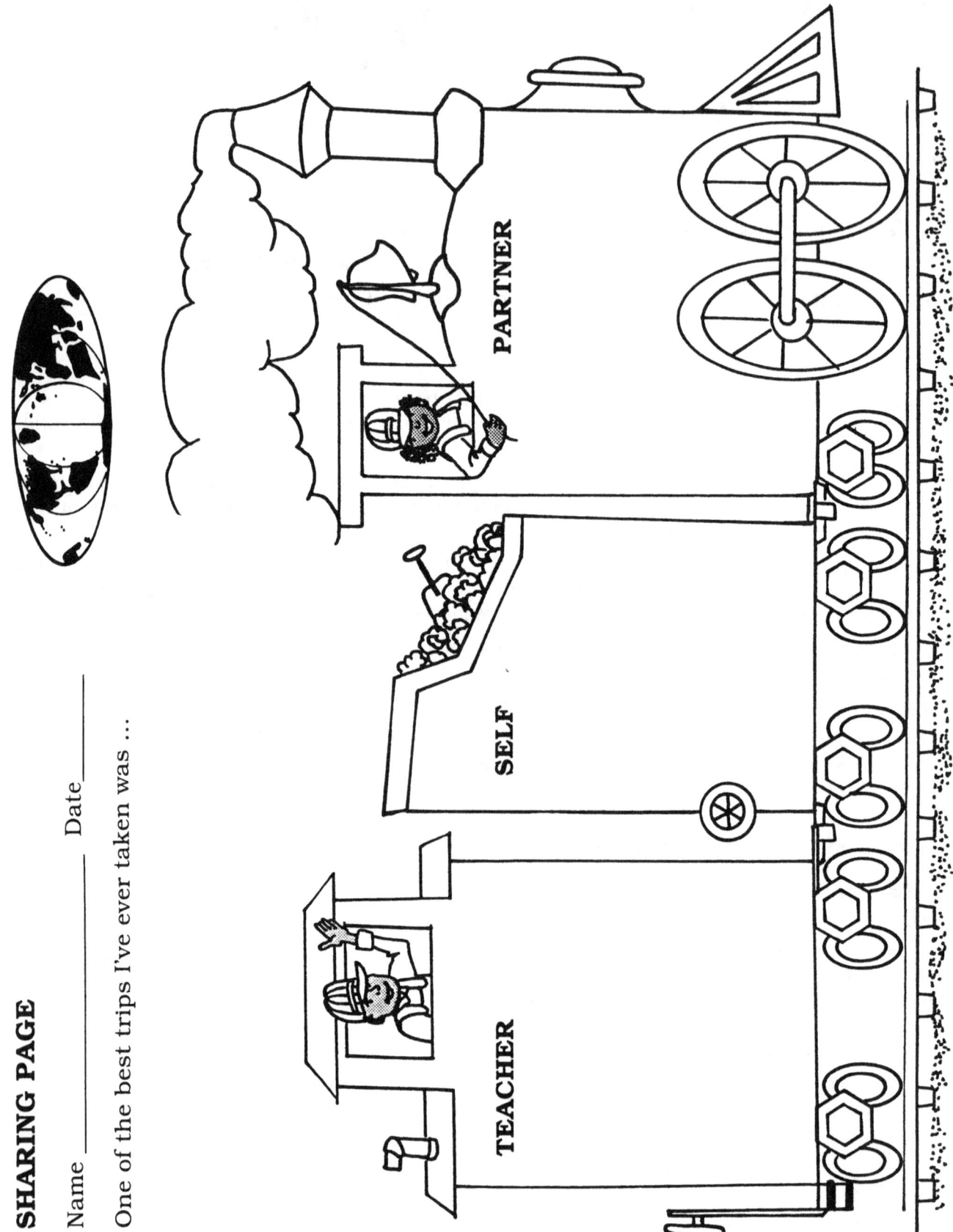

From *Practical Portfolios*. ©1994. Teacher Ideas Press, P.O. Box 6633, Englewood, CO 80155-6633.

Lesson 10—Sharing Page / 55

SHARING PAGE

Name _____ Date _____

Something I appreciate in a friend is ...

From *Practical Portfolios.* ©1994. Teacher Ideas Press, P.O. Box 6633, Englewood, CO 80155-6633.

56 / 3—Suggested First-of-the-Year Portfolio Lessons

SHARING PAGE

Name _____ Date _____

Three things I really like about myself are …

PARTNER

SELF

TEACHER

From *Practical Portfolios*. ©1994. Teacher Ideas Press, P.O. Box 6633, Englewood, CO 80155-6633.

LESSON 11—LEARNING STYLES

Objective

Students will understand learning styles and how knowledge of learning styles is beneficial. Students will take a learning style inventory.

Note: You should use the learning style theory and inventory with which you are familiar and comfortable. This lesson gives general information to include. You may want to allow two or three days for this lesson, depending on the amount of detail included on learning styles.

Preparation

1. Choose and duplicate a learning style inventory of your choice.

2. Prepare examples of your own learning style. Include methods you use to help you learn new information, how you organize yourself, what characteristics you have that indicate your learning style, and so on. It is also helpful to give examples of other adults you know with other learning styles. This enables students to see that there are many different styles and that all are acceptable.

Content

1. Discuss learning styles. Each person has a distinct method of acquiring new knowledge that works best and produces the desired result of learning. This is an individual's learning style. Research has shown that students can learn more effectively and efficiently and retain information longer if they are instructed using approaches that complement their learning styles (Carbo, Dunn, and Dunn 1986, 2). Students can help themselves study and learn by becoming aware of their own learning styles. Acquiring new knowledge is an important life skill, and students will benefit from understanding the most effective techniques for studying and learning.

2. Give examples of your own learning style and how this knowledge is beneficial to you. For example, knowing that you are a kinesthetic learner, you plan to study and learn new information by using games or flash cards rather than sitting and just reading the material.

3. Introduce the learning style inventory of your choice. Emphasize that there are no right or wrong answers. Each question needs to be thought about carefully and answered truthfully to ensure a valid result.

4. Administer the learning style inventory. Score as indicated in the instructions. Discuss the results and how the results can be used in everyday studying and learning.

5. Collect inventories for teacher review. Place them in the Life Skills section at the next scheduled portfolio time.

LESSON 12—APPLICATIONS FOR CLASSROOM JOBS

Objective

Students will understand and use the guidelines for completing an application.

Preparation

1. Duplicate the application on page 59 using the Life Skills color.
2. Prepare an overhead transparency of the application.
3. Obtain a blank overhead transparency.
4. Decide on the classroom jobs for which students will apply.

Content

1. Explain the guidelines for completing an application, using a blank overhead transparency. Record your points as you discuss them to enable students to refer to them when completing the application. Applications should be neatly printed except for signature, answers should be complete and truthful, and all questions should be answered. If an answer does not apply, the letters "N A" should be used in the blank for "not applicable."
2. Discuss the classroom jobs and the qualifications for each.
3. Explain the terminology on the application using the prepared overhead:

    Position desired: Give the title of the job for which you are applying.
    Qualifications: List all your experience and personal qualities.
    Education: Write in the name of your current school.
    References: Give the name of an adult, not a relative, who knows your work abilities.
    Signature: Write your name in cursive, which indicates you have given honest answers on the application.

4. Have students complete the application.
5. Review the applications. Use the completed applications to assign classroom jobs at the beginning of the year. (The jobs will actually rotate throughout the year with students having the opportunity to do each job.) Place them in the Life Skills section of the portfolio during Lesson 18.

Suggested Other Uses for Applications

Peer tutor, playground conflict mediator, teacher assistant, safety patrol, drama auditions, checking account for reward system

APPLICATION

Remember to follow these rules:

1. Always print or type neatly except for the signature line.
2. Never leave any blank spaces. Write "N A" for "not applicable" if the question does not apply to you.

Name_____ Date_____

Address_____

City_____ State_____ Zip _____

Phone_____ Position Desired_____

List your qualifications. (These tell the interviewer what you do well. Examples can be general, as in fast learner and responsible, or can be specific to the job, such as neat handwriting for recording lunch count.)

_____

_____

_____

List the experience you have that will help you do this job. (Be sure to include volunteer work, babysitting, yard work, household chores, pet care, etc.)

_____

_____

_____

Education
School: _____ How many years?_____

Reference: (One adult, not a relative, who knows you are a good worker. Ask this person for permission to be your reference.)

_____

My signature indicates all the statements on this application are true.

Signature _____

From *Practical Portfolios.* ©1994. Teacher Ideas Press, P.O. Box 6633, Englewood, CO 80155-6633.

LESSON 13—INTERVIEW SKILLS

Objective

Students will demonstrate important interview skills by completing an interview with an adult.

Preparation

Plan a time in your schedule for interviewing each student. Parent volunteers might help with this activity.

Content

1. Explain why interview skills are important to learn. Interviews are required of most job applicants, for some school admissions, and for consideration for some memberships or awards. Interviews enable another person to learn more about the candidate's qualifications and suitability for the position. The candidate has one opportunity to make a favorable impression and must be well prepared.

2. Give examples of skills needed for a successful interview. (See the rubric standard on p. 61.)

3. Brainstorm other ideas for a successful interview.

4. Create a standard of proficiency for an interview. Then develop the "novice," "emerging," and "exceeds standard" categories. Type and duplicate this rubric for scoring during individual interviews.

5. Brainstorm possible questions that might be asked in an interview. The following are some examples: Why do you want this job? What experience do you have? What are your strengths and weaknesses? Why are you the best candidate for this job? What are your qualifications? What do you do in your free time?

6. Ask for two volunteers to do a mock interview for the class, using the questions prepared by the class.

7. Have students complete practice interviews with partners.

8. Have students complete interviews for class jobs during the next several days. Explain that the interviews and applications are for practice. Most students will rotate through the different class jobs, rather than a few students holding all the jobs for the entire year.

9. Save each student's interview rating page for placement in the Life Skills section during Lesson 18.

Interview Rubric

EXCEEDS STANDARD **EX**	I prepare a résumé. I obtain letters of reference. I do all the items in the standard.
STANDARD **ST**	I dress appropriately. I arrive on time for the interview. I prepare for possible interview questions. I make eye contact with the interviewer. I answer questions with complete information. I speak clearly. I do not chew gum.
EMERGING **EM**	I dress carelessly. I am slightly late for the interview. I do very little preparation for possible questions. I look down frequently during the interview. I do not elaborate on answers. I speak softly so that the interviewer has difficulty hearing me. I chew gum.
NOVICE **NO**	I wear an inappropriate outfit. I am extremely late for the interview. I do not prepare for possible questions. I do not make eye contact with the interviewer. I give simple "yes" and "no" answers. When I speak, the interviewer can't hear me. I chew gum.

From *Practical Portfolios*. ©1994. Teacher Ideas Press, P.O. Box 6633, Englewood, CO 80155-6633.

LESSON 14—READING SURVEY

Objective

Students will complete reading surveys.

Preparation

Duplicate the Reading Survey (see p. 63) or another of your choice. Use the color you have designated for the Reading section.

Content

1. Explain that a survey has no right or wrong answers. Ask students to answer truthfully and to take time to think answers through carefully.//
2. Explain that the surveys will be used to help students learn more about their interests and attitudes in reading.
3. Distribute the surveys. Read and discuss each question. Allow time for thinking and writing.
4. Collect the surveys. Review answers to become more aware of students' reading interests and attitudes. When portfolios are assembled, redistribute the surveys for placement in the Reading section during Lesson 18.

Name _____ Date _____

READING SURVEY

1. Do you like to read?_____ Why or why not?_____
   _____
   _____

2. How many books did you read during the past year?_____
3. What are your favorite types of books?_____
   _____

4. How often do you read magazines or newspapers?_____
5. Which magazines and sections of the newspaper do you like the most?_____
   _____

6. Who are the authors you really like?_____
   _____
   _____

7. Do you check out books from the public library?_____ If yes, how often?_____
   _____

8. Do you buy books or magazines to read?_____ If yes, how often?_____
   _____

9. How often do you read outside of school? (Circle one. This includes books, magazines, newspapers, scout or hobby books, etc.)

   almost every day   once a week   rarely

10. What are some reading strategies used by good readers?_____
    _____
    _____
    _____

11. What does a student have to do to be a good reader?_____
    _____
    _____

12. Do or did your parents read to you?_____ If yes, how often?_____
    _____

13. Should the teacher read aloud to the class?_____ If yes, what books do you suggest?_____

14. How often do your parents read at home? (Circle one.)

    every day   once a week   rarely

From *Practical Portfolios*. ©1994. Teacher Ideas Press, P.O. Box 6633, Englewood, CO 80155-6633.

LESSON 15—WRITING SURVEY

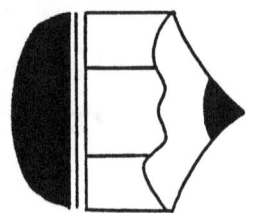

Objective

Students will complete writing surveys.

Preparation

Duplicate the Writing Survey in this guidebook (see p. 65) or one of your choice. Use the color you have designated for the Writing section.

Content

1. Explain that the Writing Survey is similar to the Reading Survey and has no right or wrong answers. The students need to answer truthfully and take time to think answers through carefully.

2. Explain that the surveys will be used to help students and teachers learn more about their writing attitudes and opinions.

3. Distribute the surveys. Read and discuss each question. Allow time for thinking and writing.

4. Collect the surveys. Review answers to become more aware of students' writing attitudes and opinions. After portfolios are assembled, redistribute the surveys for placement in the Writing section during Lesson 18.

Name _____ Date _____

WRITING SURVEY

1. Name some different types of writing a person may do._____
   _____
   _____
   _____

2. Why should you learn to write?_____
   _____
   _____
   _____

3. Do you consider yourself to be a writer?_____ Explain your answer.
   _____
   _____
   _____

4. Do you like to write?_____ Why or why not?_____
   _____
   _____
   _____

5. What are some strategies you use to help you write?_____
   _____
   _____
   _____

6. Where do you get your ideas for writing?_____
   _____
   _____
   _____

7. How does reading help you to become a better writer?_____
   _____
   _____
   _____

8. What makes a piece of writing "good"?_____
   _____
   _____
   _____

From *Practical Portfolios*. ©1994. Teacher Ideas Press, P.O. Box 6633, Englewood, CO 80155-6633.

LESSON 16—MATH SKILLS DEMONSTRATION

Objective

Students will demonstrate their understanding of math concepts in 13 areas.

Preparation

1. Duplicate Math Skills Demonstration page in the color designated for the Math section. (See p. 67.)
2. Prepare a transparency of the Math Skills Demonstration page.
3. Prepare example problems for each of the 13 areas.

Content

1. Distribute the Math Skills Demonstration page.
2. Name the 13 skill areas of math and give an example problem for each.
3. Explain that the students will create their own problems for each math skill. They should make the problems as difficult as they can to demonstrate all of their knowledge. This is not intended to be a math lesson. If the students do not understand a concept, that area of the Math Skills Demonstration page should be left blank. Students can use the back if more room is needed.
4. Allow time for work.
5. There are several options for checking the students' work. For computation problems, students might switch papers and check each other's work using the calculator. Problems requiring writing and drawing can be checked in a similar manner, or you may check these yourself. Place small sticky notes next to any problems requiring corrections. Students leave the sticky notes in place so that when the problems are rechecked, it is not necessary to review the entire paper. If it is obvious that the student does not understand the concept, that particular area does not need to be reworked at this time.
6. Save and place these papers in the Math section during Lesson 18.

Lesson 16—Math Skills Demonstration / 67

Name_____ Date_____ GR.___

MATH SKILLS DEMONSTRATION

1. One of the most important Math Life Skills is estimation. 　Example: 　44　　　　40 　+31　　　+30 　　　　　　70

2. I learn to read numbers so I can write numbers on checks, and so on. Write a number; then write the same number using words.

3. I know place value so I can read and understand numbers. Write a number. Then draw an arrow to one of the digits and label its place value.

4. I can do addition	5. Subtraction
6. I can do multiplication	7. Division

8. This is an example of a universal set and 2 subsets U = { ? } and 2 subsets equal { ? } , { ? }

9. I can do Life Skill problem solving. Write a problem about everyday happenings that involve math; then solve the problem. For example, show how to divide a pizza among four friends and name each part.

10. I can do these operations on the calculator: 　Example: 　I push 3 then + then 4 then = to get 7 　I push ___ then ___ then ___ then ___ to get _____

11. This is what I understand about measurement _____ Using your ruler, mark and label the line above.	12. Time 　　　◯ Draw a clock with a time on it and label the time.

13. This is what I understand about 　Fractions_____ 　Draw and label and/or do a problem.	Geometry_____ Draw and label.

From *Practical Portfolios*. ©1994. Teacher Ideas Press, P.O. Box 6633, Englewood, CO 80155-6633.

LESSON 17—COMPUTER DEMONSTRATION

Objective

Students will choose a sample of their computer work and write brief notes on the skills needed to complete the project.

Preparation

Have students print out a computer project of their choice.

Content

1. Distribute computer projects.
2. Have students brainstorm the skills they needed to complete the computer project.
3. Have students record the skills they used on the computer project. For example, below a computer picture, a student might write the following:

    For this project I needed to know
    a. How to set a shape
    b. How to draw lines
    c. How to "stamp"
    d. How to "fill"

4. Have students three-hole punch their computer projects and place them in the Life Skills section of their portfolios.

4 Organizing Work into Portfolios, Writing Summaries, and Goals

LESSON 18—ORGANIZING FIRST-OF-THE-YEAR WORK INTO PORTFOLIOS AND MAKING FIRST VIP ENTRIES

Objective

Students will organize items into the portfolios and make the first VIP entries.

Preparation

1. Save and three-hole punch student work to be included in the portfolios.
2. Collect a reading book from each student and photocopy one page from each book.

Content

1. Distribute completed student work that is suitable for the portfolios. Have the students place this work in the designated sections. Examples of work to be included have been presented in chapter 3. Other ideas are listed on the title pages for each section.
2. Have students place the Home Responsibility Inventory in the portfolio at this time.
3. Return reading books with photocopies to the students. Have students date and three-hole punch the reading page for placement in the Reading section.
4. Turn to the VIP section. Explain that students may write down any important achievements or activities that are not included in other sections of the portfolio. See page 70 for examples of VIP ideas. Students then write their VIP entries under Student Comments. (See sample student VIP page on p. 71.)

Idea Page for VIP Entries

Selected as teacher assistant
Selected as peer tutor
Did all my chores without being asked
Received a new puppy for my birthday/Trained my dog to do a new trick
Received a letter from my grandmother
Went to visit my grandpa and grandma
Earned next belt in tae kwon do or karate
Learned how to build a birdhouse
Finished the longest book I've ever read
Earned $10 babysitting this weekend
Started staying up until 9:00 P.M. on school nights
Opened a savings account
Went alone to the grocery store with a list from my mom
Made a new friend
Got a new haircut that is really rad
Learned to do a flip on the tramp
Got my highest score on Mario Brothers
Went to space camp or scout camp
Started volunteering at the nursing home
Learned how to do a good interview
Tried to water ski
Went horseback riding for the first time
Made my mom a special Valentine card
Learned how to braid hair
Went on a trip to_____
Figured out the science experiment
Went to the dentist and had no cavities
Did my first dive off the high dive
Learned to find a constellation in the sky by myself
Figured out a new program in computer class
Finished my first latch-hook rug project
Practiced my soccer skills on my own every day
Kept my desk clean all week
Got my first S+ on handwriting/Competed in geography or spelling bee
Played in the band for the first time
Entered a contest/Won a contest/Came in ____ place in a contest
Made a soccer goal/Went to a professional sports game

From *Practical Portfolios*. ©1994. Teacher Ideas Press, P.O. Box 6633, Englewood, CO 80155-6633.

Lesson 18—Organizing First-of-the-Year Work into Portfolios and Making First VIP Entries / 71

V.I.P.

Each student may want to include in the portfolio items that do not fit in the preceding sections. This section announces the activities and events to be celebrated that are Very Important to this Person.

Examples of VIP entries are sports, music, art, contests, trips, or anything not included elsewhere in the portfolio.

STUDENT COMMENTS	VISITOR COMMENTS
9/10/92 I got to play in the basketball game every quarter last Saturday.	
- I just earned my gold Karate belt.	
10/29/92 I entered the scary Story Contest.	
11/15/92 I have been to all the meetings of Junior Great Books.	
12/10/92 I helped make 10 crafts to sell at the Girl Scout fair.	

From *Practical Portfolios*. ©1994. Teacher Ideas Press, P.O. Box 6633, Englewood, CO 80155-6633.

LESSON 19—CREATING A CLASSROOM RUBRIC FOR STUDENT PORTFOLIOS

Objective

Students will review rubrics, how they are used, and how they are created. Students will create a Rubric for Student Portfolio Expectations.

Preparation

Gather examples of rubrics and make overhead transparencies. (See pp. 44-49.)

Content

1. Review the term rubric. (See p. 43.)
2. Give several examples of rubrics, using the overhead transparencies.
3. Explain that the class will create a Rubric for Portfolio Expectations.
4. Brainstorm requirements for a good portfolio. (See example on p. 73.)
5. List these ideas as the standard.
6. Develop the "novice," "emerging," and "exceeds standard" categories.

Post Preparation

Type the Rubric for Portfolio Expectations. Students place the rubric in the portfolio behind the Visitor Log during a scheduled portfolio time.

Rubric for Portfolio Expectations

EXCEEDS STANDARD
EX
- I follow all characteristics of the standard.
- I write more than one goal per area each quarter.
- I demonstrate insight and depth of thinking on my summaries and reflections.

STANDARD
ST
- I write realistic, short-term goals.
- I write one goal per area each quarter.
- I keep my portfolio neatly organized and free of extra marks.
- I write clearly and neatly.
- I write thoughtfully and carefully on my summaries and reflections.
- I continue to select work samples, at least one per subject each quarter.
- I independently decide when goals are met and complete the goal-attainment forms.
- I follow all teacher instructions for portfolio work.

EMERGING
EM
- I write goals, but they are vague and unclear.
- I write less than one goal per area each quarter.
- My work in each portfolio section is not organized; I have some unnecessary writing on the pages.
- Some of my writing is difficult to read.
- I write my summaries and reflections without careful thought.
- I need reminders to select ongoing samples of work.
- I need reminders to evaluate goals and complete the goal-attainment forms.
- Sometimes I don't pay attention to the instructions for portfolio work.

NOVICE
NO
- I only write goals with help and reminders.
- My work is located in the wrong section of the portfolio; I doodle and draw inappropriately on portfolio pages.
- My writing is difficult to read.
- I do not write summaries and reflections without help.
- I do not select work without help from the teacher.
- I do not evaluate goals or complete the forms without help.
- I frequently miss the teacher's instructions for portfolio work.

LESSON 20—FIRST WRITING SAMPLE

Objective

Students will understand the writing sample expectations for their grade level and receive the completed Creative Writing Checklists for their stories. (Teacher may use their own district guidelines for this lesson.) Students will graph the results of this writing sample.

Preparation

1. Complete a Creative Writing Checklist for each student's story. (See pp. 78-79.) Place a check on the line before each skill demonstrated by a student. The highest level for which a student demonstrates all the characteristics indicates the student's writing level. However, if a student demonstrates some characteristics in one grade level and some in the next grade level, that student is achieving somewhere between the two grade levels. If your school district has criteria for your grade level, these may be substituted for the criteria checklist. Although awareness of general grade level expectations is important, these are simply guidelines to help teachers and students set realistic goals. For example, a student who writes stories with complete main ideas would then work on developing the main idea more fully and describing characters and setting. (See "Ideas" column on p. 78.)

2. When evaluating a story, include one or two areas of strength and one or two suggestions for improvement of future pieces. (See sample summary on p. 86.) We recommend that comments be written on a self-adhesive label and stapled to the story with the backing still intact. The students then peel off the label and stick it to the summary column on the Writing title page. This eliminates the need for you to recopy the writing comments onto the title page.

3. Prepare overhead transparencies of the Creative Writing Checklist and sample student paper.

4. Duplicate the Writing Sample cover on page 76, the Visitor Information on page 77, and the Creative Writing Checklist Graph on pages 80 and 81, using the color of paper selected for the Writing section.

Content

1. Explain the wide variation in student levels. Every student will have relative strengths and areas for improvement. Distribute and discuss the Visitor Information page.

2. Distribute stories and completed checklists to the students. Using the overhead transparencies of the checklist and a sample student paper, explain the Creative Writing Checklist.

3. Emphasize that students will be working on their skills throughout the year. All students are working at different levels but are expected to show growth from their starting point by the end of the year.

4. Have students decide on their best area and mark it with a star.

5. Have students choose the area or areas they feel need the most improvement and mark them with "needs work."

6. Distribute the graph. Students color in the bars for the first writing sample to visually indicate the writing characteristics they have demonstrated.

7. Have students remove the backing from the self-adhesive label and place the label in the summary column of the Writing title page. Instruct the students to write the date in the column provided.

8. Have students complete the information on the Writing Sample cover.

9. Place the Visitor Information page, Writing Sample cover, checklist, story, and graph in the Writing section of the portfolio.

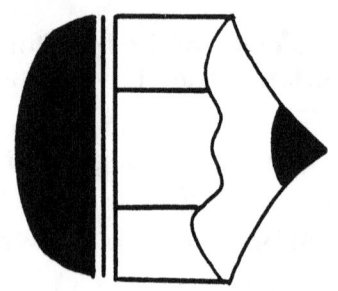

WRITING SAMPLE #__

DATE_____

TITLE:_____

_____

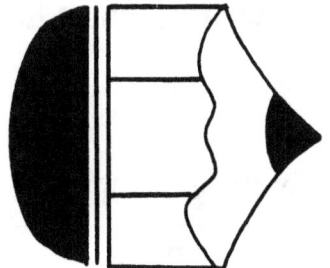

Visitors to the Portfolio

Please Note the Information Below:

The following pages are a Creative Writing Checklist. The purpose of this checklist is to have reference points of general characteristics in writing and to allow students and teachers to set goals and plan instruction. It is very important to understand that each child is unique and few children are at their exact grade level in each of the seven areas. Keep in mind that the characteristics stated at each level should ideally be demonstrated at the end of the grade level identified on the left side. Also, this is just one writing sample, and students may demonstrate different levels of proficiency on different writing samples. Checkmarks indicate writing characteristics the student is currently demonstrating. Evidence of success is determined by the growth demonstrated by each individual student, rather than comparing the student to a group.

78 / 4—Organizing Work into Portfolios, Writing Summaries, and Goals

Creative Writing Checklist Part 1

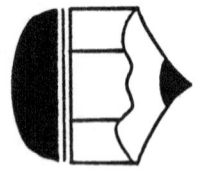

Name _____ Writing Sample #____ Title:_____

GRADE LEVEL	IDEAS	PARAGRAPH ORGANIZATION	SENTENCE STRUCTURE
7	__Imaginative story idea __Logical beginning and ending	Paragraphs have __Purpose __Narrow topic __Supporting details __Closing sentences __Multiple paragraphs are written in order of importance	

6	__Logical development	__Some change of paragraph with change of speaker
		__Clear beginning, middle, and end
		__Endings sometimes creative but abrupt
			__Complete sentences
			__4 sentence patterns:
			  __noun-verb
			  __noun-verb-noun
			  __noun-linking verb-noun
			  __noun-linking verb-adjective

5	__Developed main idea __Developed characters __Imaginative settings	__Paragraph sentences sometimes sequenced __Clear beginning and end __Related title __Logical progression	__Minimal run-ons and fragments __Simple, compound, complex sentences evident
4	__Main idea __Somewhat developed idea	__Some single-idea paragraphs	__Many types of sentences __Some variety in sentence patterns __Occasional run-ons and fragments
3	__Communicates an idea __Has a direction __Creative title	__Usually 1 paragraph __Some abrupt endings	__Simple sentences with subject-verb __Some run-ons __Some variety in types of sentences
2	__Has a beginning __Several unrelated ideas __Some direction	__Sequence usually evident	__Simple sentences, often complete __Run-ons __Fragments
1	__Concrete	__Sequence of events sometimes apparent	__Simple sentences, some complete __Run-ons __Fragments

Credit to Jefferson County Public Schools

From *Practical Portfolios*. ©1994. Teacher Ideas Press, P.O. Box 6633, Englewood, CO 80155-6633.

Creative Writing Checklist Part 2

GRADE LEVEL	STYLE AND VOCABULARY	USAGE AND GRAMMAR	MECHANICS	SPELLING
7	__Personal choice of words, sentences, and paragraphs	__Generally correct	__Generally correct	__7th-grade words usually correct
6	__Higher vocabulary __Effective adjectives and adverbs __Consistent point of view	__Tries variety of verb tenses __Generally correct homonym usage	__Some common errors __Dialogue correct	__Irregular words sometimes misspelled __6th-grade words usually correct
5	__Appropriate adjectives and adverbs __Consistent point of view __Variety of word choices and descriptions	__Generally correct	__Commas sometimes overused __Other punctuation correct	__Misspelling generally phonetic __Fewer prefix and suffix errors __5th-grade words usually correct
4	__Occasional basic words __Some variety of words __Tries sensory description	__Correct verb forms __Generally correct pronouns	__Paragraph indentation __Basic capitals correct __Dialogue sometimes correct	__Some prefix and suffix errors __Some ending errors __4th-grade words usually correct
3	__Basic vocabulary __Few modifiers __Simple description	__Some pronouns __No double negatives __Subject-verb agreement __Correct verb forms	__Some paragraph indentation __Capitalizes first word in sentence __Ending punctuation __Simple contraction __Dialogue tried	__Some phonetic misspellings __3rd-grade words usually correct
2	__No description __Simple, appropriate vocabulary	__Tries pronouns __Some subject-verb agreement __Usually present and past tenses	__Sentences usually capitalized __Random use of other punctuation	__Many errors __Tries CVC/CVVC __2nd-grade words usually correct
1	__Repetitive lists __No description __Simple vocabulary	__Present and past tenses sometimes correct	__Occasional use of capitals and periods	__Many errors __Low sound-symbol relationship

From *Practical Portfolios*. ©1994. Teacher Ideas Press, P.O. Box 6633, Englewood, CO 80155-6633.

Creative Writing Checklist Graph Part 1

Name _____ Date of 1st color _____ Date of 2nd color _____

GRADE LEVEL	IDEAS		PARAGRAPH ORGANIZATION		SENTENCE STRUCTURE	
	1st sample	3rd sample	1st sample	3rd sample	1st sample	3rd sample
7						
6						
5						
4						
3						
2						
1						

From *Practical Portfolios.* ©1994. Teacher Ideas Press, P.O. Box 6633, Englewood, CO 80155-6633.

Creative Writing Checklist Graph Part 2

GRADE LEVEL	STYLE AND VOCABULARY		USAGE AND GRAMMAR		MECHANICS		SPELLING	
	1st sample	3rd sample	1st sample	3rd sample	1st sample	3rd sample	1st sample	3rd sample
7								
6								
5								
4								
3								
2								
1								

From *Practical Portfolios*. ©1994. Teacher Ideas Press, P.O. Box 6633, Englewood, CO 80155-6633.

LESSON 21—COMPOSING READING AND WRITING GOALS

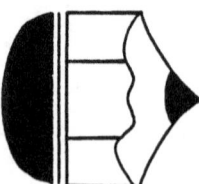

Objective

Students will write goals for the Reading and Writing sections of the portfolio.

Preparation

1. Record the Reading summary for each student. (See summary column on p. 85.) Summaries should include one or two areas of strength and one or two areas for improvement, based upon teacher observation and information from student-teacher reading conferences. Writing summaries were added to the portfolio in the previous lesson when students placed the self-adhesive labels on the Writing title pages.

2. Duplicate copies of color-coded Reading and Writing Goals. These are for reference only and do not need to be three-hole punched. (See pp. 83-84.)

Content

1. Turn to Reading section of the portfolio. Each student reads the summary completed by the teacher.

2. Distribute the page of Sample Reading Goals. Discuss possible goals for this section, which may be based on but are not limited to the Sample Goals. Goals may also be based directly on the comments in the teacher summary. Stress that goals should be realistic and short-term.

3. Have students write one or two goals on the Reading title page in the goals section. (See goals column on p. 85.)

4. Repeat steps 1–3 for the Writing section. Sample writing goals are on page 84. A sample Writing title page with teacher summary and student goals is on page 86.

Reading Goals

1. I will read _____ pages in books of my own choice this quarter.
2. I will have a book to read during each reading class.
3. I will read at home _____ days a week.
4. I will read a book that is a different kind of literature from what I usually read.
5. I will read other books by authors I like.
6. I will read books recommended to me by others.
7. I will not keep reading a book that I am not enjoying. I will give the author _____ chapters before I stop and try a different book.
8. I will read a book that is challenging to me.
9. I will assess the difficulty of my book by using the five-finger method. (That is, if I don't know five or more words on a page, the book may be too difficult for me.)
10. I will read to understand the meaning of the story, trying not to read word by word.
11. I will tell my thoughts and opinions more in my journal instead of just writing about the plot.
12. I will write in complete thoughts for my journal entries, story maps, and book projects.
13. I will describe the characters completely on my story maps by telling both physical and personality characteristics.
14. I will demonstrate understanding of vocabulary words by completing the assigned vocabulary activities appropriately.
15. My book projects will show logical development from statement of problems, through events, to solutions.
16. My book projects will explain the story in enough detail to be easily understood by others.
17. I will create book projects of my own design.
18. When reading nonfiction, I will preview by reading chapter titles and headings and looking at pictures and charts.
19. I will ignore distractions and not talk to others during silent reading.
20. I will remain seated in one spot and read silently for a half hour.
21. I will share my thoughts and opinions about my book during reading discussions.

From *Practical Portfolios.* ©1994. Teacher Ideas Press, P.O. Box 6633, Englewood, CO 80155-6633.

Writing Goals

1. I will brainstorm topics and choose the best ones for my writing.
2. I will keep a list of possible writing topics and add to the list as I think of ideas.
3. I will work on focus by concentrating on the most important part of my story.
4. I will make plans for my stories by mapping, completing story maps, webbing, and so on.
5. I will make my settings more real by using sensory description.
6. I will describe the characters in my stories, telling both physical and personality characteristics.
7. I will remember to "show" the action in my stories.
8. I will notice how professional authors write and will use their techniques in my stories.
9. I will listen carefully in conferences and make decisions about revisions.
10. I will listen to the stories of others and make helpful comments.
11. I will follow the rules for conferring with peers.
12. I will revise my writing to make the meaning clearer.
13. I will proofread my stories for word choice, omitted words, and missing word endings.
14. I will proofread my stories for punctuation.
15. I will proofread for spelling by circling the words I think are misspelled. I will correct words.
16. I will indent paragraphs for changes in topic, time, or place.
17. I will indent for each new speaker when writing direct quotes.
18. I will punctuate beginnings and endings of sentences consistenty.
19. I will work on handwriting by (writing neatly, forming letters correctly, connecting letters correctly, etc.).
20. I will remember to use commas in compound sentences.
21. I will punctuate the direct words of a speaker correctly.
22. I will share my writing with others.
23. I will ignore distractions and not disturb others.
24. I will use my writing time wisely.

From *Practical Portfolios*. ©1994. Teacher Ideas Press, P.O. Box 6633, Englewood, CO 80155-6633.

Lesson 21—Composing Reading and Writing Goals / 85

READING

This section gives an overview of student abilities in all areas of the reading process. Suggested items to include are

Reading surveys completed by the student
An ongoing list of books and genres read by the student
Photocopies of different reading book pages
Sample reading journal entries (literature response)
Teacher anecdotal records
Notes of conferences between teacher and student
Any checklists used in reading
Reflections on the year's achievements and activities in reading

The area below is provided for periodic synthesis and summarization of portfolio data in order to look at past and future goals. Synthesis is a critical component of portfolio assessment. It should be done on a regular basis and should include the student

DATE	SUMMARY	DATE	GOALS	DATE ATTAINED
9/15	Good discussion of story elements. Need to work on completing vocabulary activities	9/20	I will complete the vocabulary activities for my reading.	OK 10/27 KD
10/25	Vocabulary activities much improved. Need to work on more complete book projects.	10/27	I will make my book projects more complete.	
		10/27	I will read a book that is challenging to me.	

From *Practical Portfolios*. ©1994. Teacher Ideas Press, P.O. Box 6633, Englewood, CO 80155-6633.

This section includes many types of writing and may include pieces in various stages of the writing process. Suggested items to include are

Writing surveys completed by the student
Drafts and final copies of expository, creative, and persuasive writing
Social studies and science reports
Research papers
Anecdotal records and conference records
Handwriting and spelling work
Reflections on the year's achievements and activities in writing
Functional writing such as checks, applications, letters, invitations, lists, picture captions, articles, and so on.
District writing checklist

The area below is provided for periodic synthesis and summarization of portfolio data in order to look at past and future goals. Synthesis is a critical component to portfolio assessment. It should be done on a regular basis and should include the student.

DATE	SUMMARY	DATE	GOALS	DATE ATTAINED
9/18	Strengths in development of ideas and grammar. Need to develop characters and settings.	9/20	I will describe my characters and settings more.	OK 10/30 KD
		9/20	I will follow peer conferencing rules.	OK 10/30 KD
10/29	Improvement seen in development of characters and settings. Need to work on punctuation of quotes.	10/30	I will punctuate quotes in my stories	

From *Practical Portfolios*. ©1994. Teacher Ideas Press, P.O. Box 6633, Englewood, CO 80155-6633.

LESSON 22—STUDENT SUMMARY WRITING FOR LIFE SKILLS AND MATH

Objective

Students will write summaries of their skills for Life Skills and Math.

Students write their own summaries for these sections of the portfolio for the following reasons:

1. This activity gives the students time to reflect on their life skills and math skills development.
2. Students learn the skill of summary writing.
3. This activity greatly reduces the time required by the teacher for maintaining the portfolios.

Preparation

1. Duplicate the Idea Pages for Life Skills and Math Summaries. (See pp. 88, 90.)
2. The Home Responsibility Inventory and the Math Skills Demonstration page were placed in the portfolio in Lesson 18.

Content

1. Explain that a summary states important points clearly and concisely. Give examples of how to choose main points in summarizing.
2. Turn to the Life Skills section. Review the meaning of life skills and what is to be included in this area. (See p. 89.) Distribute the Idea Page for Life Skills Summaries and discuss the examples. For additional information, refer students to the Home Responsibility Inventory that parents completed at the beginning of the year.
3. Have students reflect on their current abilities in life skills.
4. Have students write their Life Skills summaries using the format on page 88. A sample student Life Skills summary is written in the summary column on page 89.
5. Turn to the Math section. Distribute the Idea Page for Math Summaries and discuss the examples. Review the Math Skills Demonstration page that students completed in Lesson 16.
6. Have students reflect on their math abilities.
7. Have students write their Math summaries, using the format on page 90. A sample student Math summary is written in the summary column on page 91.

Idea Page for Life Skills Summaries

In writing your life skills summary, you will need to complete sentences similar to the following:

My strengths in life skills are _____
_____

I need to work on _____
_____

The following phrases are examples of items that may be used to complete the sentences for the life skills summary. You may write other items that apply to you but are not mentioned here.

SCHOOL

Personal responsibility
Completing assignments on time
Returning my weekly folder
Returning home-school
    correspondence
Daily attendance except for illness
Prompt arrival
Classroom skills
Following directions
Raising my hand before speaking
Not moving about the room unnecessarily
Being considerate of others
Working independently
Care of property
Keeping my desk neatly organized
Having my materials ready at class time
Taking home my coat, hat, and so on each
    day

Group responsibility
Listening to others' ideas
Taking turns
Contributing ideas
Sharing materials
Compromising
Encouraging others
Not criticizing others
Playground cooperation
Sharing equipment
Being a team player
Accepting group decisions
Not arguing
Computer skills
Knowledge of learning style

HOME

Responsibility
Doing my chores without reminders
Taking care of my pet
Taking care of my property

Managing my money
Considering other family members

COMMUNITY

Doing a community service project
Helping neighbors with_____

Collecting trash in _____ area
Job shadowing in _____

From *Practical Portfolios*. ©1994. Teacher Ideas Press, P.O. Box 6633, Englewood, CO 80155-6633.

LIFE SKILLS

Life skills include all the skills the student will need to be successful in life. Reading, writing, and math are among these life skills. However, each of these academic areas has a separate section in this portfolio. Suggested items to include are

Self-evaluation/monitoring records
Learning style information
Computer skills samples
Cooperative group skills
Career awareness program records
Sample application and interview records
Peer tutor and other job evaluations
Home inventories showing home responsibilities and skills of the student
Self-awareness data (interest inventories, sharing, and autobiography)

Critical thinking skills
Health and social issues
Cultural studies
Positive self-talk
Job shadow records

The area below is provided for periodic synthesis and summarization of portfolio data in order to look at past and future goals. Synthesis is a critical component of portfolio assessment. It should be done on a regular basis and should include the student.

DATE	SUMMARY	DATE	GOALS	DATE ATTAINED
9/22	My strengths in life skills are being responsible at home and school and doing all my assignments on time. I need to clean my hamster cage more often.	9/24	I will clean my hamster cage once a week	
10/30	My hamster is happier with his cage. I'm happier with the smell. I need to think about careers I'd like to job shadow.	10/30	I will think of 5 jobs I would like to visit.	

From *Practical Portfolios*. ©1994. Teacher Ideas Press, P.O. Box 6633, Englewood, CO 80155-6633.

Idea Page for Math Summaries

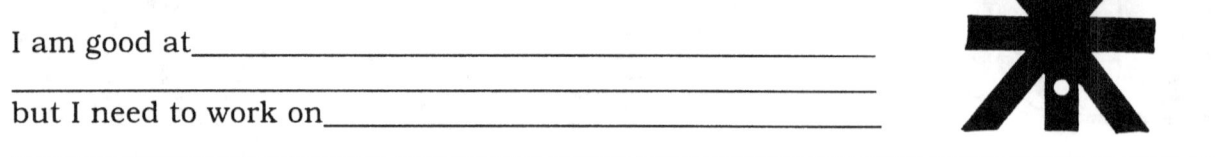

I am good at_____
_____
but I need to work on_____
_____

The following items are examples of math concepts and processes that may help you to complete your math skills summary:

place value: names of places to the_____place
decimal place value
addition
subtraction
multiplication
division
math facts: addition, subtraction, multiplication, division
estimation: addition, subtraction, multiplication, division
fractions
equivalent fractions
addition and subtraction of fractions with like denominators
addition and subtraction of fractions with unlike denominators
writing fractions in simplest terms
multiplication of fractions
division of fractions
problem solving
linear measurement (standard): measuring to the nearest inch, one-half inch, one-quarter inch, one-eighth inch, measuring by feet and yards
linear measurement (metric): measuring to the nearest millimeter, centimeter, decimeter, measuring by meters
perimeter
area
volume
addition and subtraction of measures without regrouping
addition and subtraction of measures with regrouping
circles: drawing, radius, diameter, chord
bisecting lines and angles
measurement of angles
accuracy on daily work
using math manipulatives appropriately

This section gives an overview of the student's understanding of math concepts. Suggested items to include are

Functional math records
Strategies used successfully by the student for problem solving
Sample math journal entries
Classroom work and projects
Student's personal graph for math facts progress
District checklist of math skills
Math Skills Demonstration pages

The area below is provided for periodic synthesis and summarization of portfolio data in order to look at past and future goals. Synthesis is a critical component of portfolio assessment. It should be done on a regular basis and should include the student.

DATE	SUMMARY	DATE	GOALS	DATE ATTAINED
9/22	I am good at adding and subtracting. I need to work on multiplying.	9/24	I will pass the multiplication facts.	Improving 10/29 KD
11/2	I am getting better at finding key words in life skill math problems. I need to keep working on this.	11/2	I will read a problem 2 times and circle all key words before starting to solve the problem.	

From *Practical Portfolios.* ©1994. Teacher Ideas Press, P.O. Box 6633, Englewood, CO 80155-6633.

92 / 4—Organizing Work into Portfolios, Writing Summaries, and Goals

LESSON 23—COMPOSING LIFE SKILLS AND MATH GOALS

Objective

Students will write goals for the Life Skills and Math sections of the portfolio.

Preparation

Duplicate copies of color-coded Life Skills and Math Goals. (See pp. 93, 94.) Do not three-hole punch them because they are for reference only.

Content

1. Turn to the Life Skills section of the portfolio. Have students read the summaries they wrote in the previous lesson.

2. Distribute the Life Skills Goals page. Discuss the possible goals for this section. Goals may be drawn from the sample goals or based on the student summary. Again, stress that goals should be realistic and short-term.

3. Have students write one or two life skills goals on the Life Skills title page. (See goals column on p. 89.)

4. Turn to the Math section and repeat steps 1 through 3, using the Math Goals page. (See goals column on p. 91.)

Life Skills Goals

1. I will show more responsibility at _____ by doing _____.
2. I will show growth in cooperative learning by _____ (listening more, compromising more, speaking up more, encouraging others more, etc.).
3. I will increase my computer knowledge by _____.
4. I will increase my computer level-of-comfort by _____.
5. I will increase my classroom skills by _____ (following directions, staying in my seat, listening, raising my hand, being considerate of others, etc.).
6. I will remember and use my knowledge about my learning style by _____.
7. I will arrive at school on time daily.
8. I will attend school daily except for illness.
9. I will bring my homework, folder, and other materials daily.
10. I will keep my personal property neatly organized.
11. I will complete assignments on time.
12. I will ask for help after I have asked myself at least two times and can't figure out what to do.
13. I will think of ____ good things about myself each day.
14. I will find out how each new thing I learn in school will help me in my life. I will do this by _____.
15. I will work on improving my interpersonal relationships with my peers by _____.
16. I will work on solving a problem on the playground by _____.
17. I will do my chores at home without being asked.
18. I will feed my pet every day.
19. I will manage my allowance better by _____.

From *Practical Portfolios*. ©1994. Teacher Ideas Press, P.O. Box 6633, Englewood, CO 80155-6633.

Math Goals

1. I will pass the math skills at level _____.
2. I will improve my accuracy on daily work.
3. I will pass _____ math facts.
4. I will ask a question when I don't understand something.
5. I will use manipulatives appropriately.
6. I will study math facts at home _____ times per week.
7. I will improve my skills in _____ (addition, subtraction, multiplication, fractions, geometry, measurement, etc.).
8. I will demonstrate my reasoning in math.
9. I will reduce my computation errors by writing my math problems neatly and working them carefully.
10. I will complete _____ extra credit pages this quarter.
11. I will solve life skills math problems by reading the problem twice and circling the key words.
12. I will teach my family something I have learned in math.
13. I will complete math warm-up every day without reminders.
14. I will practice my estimating skills to check if my answers are reasonable.

LESSON 24—REACHING YOUR GOALS

Objective

Students will understand the procedure for goal completion. Students will make individual name cards for the goal-attainment display and will understand how the classroom goal thermometer will be used.

Preparation

1. Duplicate the Reaching Your Goals form. (See p. 96.)
2. Cut tagboard cards approximately 5 x 8 inches for each student.
3. Make a three-foot thermometer, which can be colored in by single degrees as goals are reached.
4. Decide on the reward that will be earned when the class has reached 100 degrees. Choose smaller rewards for smaller increments on the thermometer. For example, for each 25 degrees, the class may have an extra recess, and for the 100-degree mark, a party may be planned.
5. Cut 1-inch paper squares from colored paper. Use a different color of paper for goals achieved in each quarter. These squares allow the teacher and the students to monitor goal attainment at a glance. The different colors show when the goals were achieved. Classroom view is on page 96.

Content

1. Distribute and discuss the Reaching Your Goals form. Emphasize that the students must show evidence of reaching goals. This may be a parent's signature, a teacher's signature, or the actual written work showing completion.
2. Distribute tagboard cards. Have students print their names in large letters and decorate the borders.
3. Explain that each time a student completes a goal, a goal square will be attached to the student's card. Display the goal cards on a classroom bulletin board.
4. Display the classroom thermometer. Explain that degrees will be colored in as goals are completed by the students.

Reaching Your Goals

Name:_____ Date:_____

Goal:_____

Explain the evidence you have that indicates your achievement of this goal. This could be a parent's signature, a teacher's signature, or your actual written work demonstrating this goal.

_____

_____

Write a new goal in your portfolio for this area. Initial here to show that you have written your new goal._____

Place this form in the goal basket for a conference with the teacher.

Teacher: Initial here after conference._____ Give student a colored square to staple to the name card.
Student: Staple the square to your name card and color in 1 degree on the thermometer. Place this page in the back pocket of your portfolio.

From *Practical Portfolios*. ©1994. Teacher Ideas Press, P.O. Box 6633, Englewood, CO 80155-6633.

5 Fall Student-Led Parent Conferences

LESSON 25—INTRODUCTION TO STUDENT-LED PARENT CONFERENCES

Objective

Students will understand the purpose of student-led parent conferences.

Preparation

Duplicate parent letter with time slot and refreshment request form. (See pp. 98-99.)

Content

Explain the purpose of student-led parent conferences as expressed in the parent letter. Emphasize conference goals, the form to request preferred conference times, and the response form for refreshment contributions. (For further information on student-led parent conferences, see pp. 6-7.)

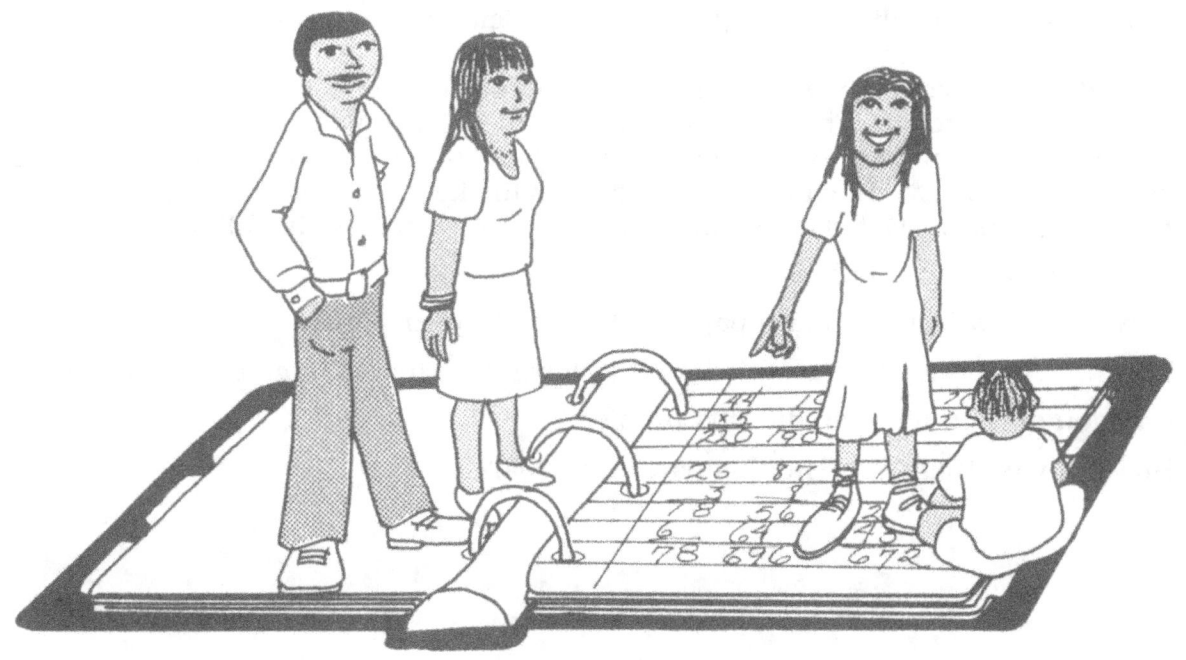

DATE_____

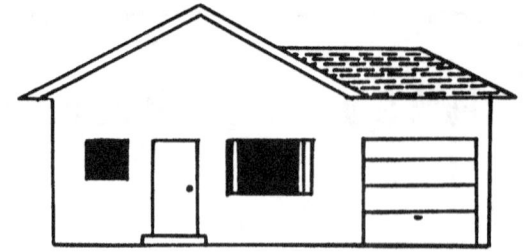

**STUDENT-LED PARENT CONFERENCES:
A CELEBRATION OF SUCCESS**

Dear Parents,

The students' portfolios are progressing very well. The students have been writing goals in the different subject areas and selecting representative samples of their work.

A format for your student to present the portfolio is the student-led parent conference. This conference will allow your student, with training, to have the central role in reporting progress. Through these conferences, students learn organization and leadership skills. They become accountable for their learning, learn to evaluate their work, and develop communication skills. We are now preparing for these conferences, which will be held at the end of this quarter.

During these conferences, your student will present work samples and discuss the items according to a planned agenda. You, as parents, will review the goals that your student has written in the Life Skills, Reading, Writing, and Math sections. Your help is needed in writing another Life Skills goal and adding ideas to the VIP section. You will also be writing a letter to your student expressing positive feedback.

Four to five conferences will take place in the room at one time. The 45-minute time block for each conference allows more time for viewing work and discussing progress than in a traditional conference. I would like to stress that your child is in charge of conducting the conference, and it is most important that we honor this role. I will be circulating from group to group, acting as a facilitator and providing clarification, if necessary.

Student-led parent conferences are meant to be celebrations of student success and demonstrations of growth. This is a time for you to express positive feelings about your student's accomplishments, rather than pointing out the errors you may see on some of the samples of work. Even though your student is in charge of the conference, your input is welcomed. Some suggested questions to ask your student are the following:

1. Where did you get this good idea for a story?
2. Why did you select this math paper to include in your portfolio?
3. How did you decide to read this book? (referring to the reading page photocopy)
4. Can you explain how you did this problem?
5. How did you decide to write this particular goal?

From *Practical Portfolios*. ©1994. Teacher Ideas Press, P.O. Box 6633, Englewood, CO 80155-6633.

Lesson 25—Introduction to Student-Led Parent Conferences / 99

Please indicate at the end of this letter your first and second time choices for the celebration with your child. I would sincerely appreciate those of you who are able to attend at any time to indicate that on the form. This would help with scheduling. If you wish to have a separate conference, times will be available from _____ to _____ P.M. on _____. I can also make arrangements before or after school for conferences at a later date. A sign-up sheet will be available for you to schedule an individual conference if you have additional questions or concerns.

I am looking forward to seeing you at our conferences/celebrations of success. Thank you for your support.

Sincerely,

* *

PLEASE RETURN BY_____.

For our celebration, I would welcome help with refreshments. Please indicate if you can contribute a dozen cookies.

____Yes, I will contribute 1 dozen cookies for the celebration.

_____PARENT SIGNATURE

PLEASE MARK YOUR FIRST AND SECOND CHOICES FOR TIMES BELOW.

If you can come at any time, check on the appropriate line.

TIME	FIRST CHOICE	SECOND CHOICE
_____	_____	_____
_____	_____	_____
_____	_____	_____
_____	_____	_____
_____	_____	_____

ANYTIME _____

COMMENTS:_____

_____

From *Practical Portfolios*. ©1994. Teacher Ideas Press, P.O. Box 6633, Englewood, CO 80155-6633.

LESSON 26—INTRODUCTION TO THE FALL CONFERENCE AGENDA

Objective

Students will become familiar with the conference agenda.

Preparation

Duplicate the Conference Agenda. (See p. 101.)

Content

1. Read through the Conference Agenda as students turn to the corresponding pages in the portfolio.
2. Silently to themselves, have students rehearse possible explanations of the agenda items.
3. Discuss student concerns and anxieties regarding the conferences. Because most students will be new to this format, they will need time to express their feelings. Many of them will be nervous. Explain that they will have several opportunities to practice their presentation. The small symbols next to each agenda item will help them remember the content of each section. The symbols will also help them keep their place on the agenda during the conference. Several of the more complicated portfolio items have written explanations.

Post Preparation

Plan the conference schedule after requests for time slots have been returned.

Fall Student-Led Parent Conference Agenda

__ 1. Make introductions if it seems to be an appropriate time. Otherwise, wait to make introductions until the teacher comes to your table. Get your reading journal and put it with your portfolio.

 __ 2. Introduce the portfolio. Ask your parents to read the front cover.

 __ 3. Show the Visitor Log. Explain that your parents will sign it at the end.

 __ 4. Show the Student Exit Outcome page, which explains the long-term goals for you upon graduation from high school.

 __ 5. Life Skills. Explain the title page. Go through each paper in this section. Write one life skills goal with your parent. There are sample goals on the table if needed. Be sure to date your goal when you write it on the title page.

 __ 6. Reading. Explain the title page and the goals you have written for yourself. Discuss the Reading Survey. Retell a little of the story that is photocopied and read a paragraph aloud to your parents. Show one entry from your reading journal and the list of books you have read.

 __ 7. Writing. Explain the title page and the goals you have written. Discuss your Writing Survey. Ask your parents to read the teacher's explanation of the Creative Writing Checklist. Show the checklist. Explain the star you marked in your best area. Discuss the area you would most like to improve. Read your story.

 __ 8. Math. Explain the title page and goals. Show the Math Skills Demonstration page and the papers you have chosen.

 __ 9. VIP. Explain anything you have included here. Ask your parents if they have other ideas and write them down.

__ 10. Parents: Write a short letter to your child expressing positives. Please place it in the Life Skills section of the portfolio. During this time, students may get refreshments and a Parent Evaluation form.

 __ 11. Have your parents sign the Visitor Log and turn in the Evaluation form.

__ 12. Thank your parents for coming. Put your portfolio away and clean up.

From *Practical Portfolios*. ©1994. Teacher Ideas Press, P.O. Box 6633, Englewood, CO 80155-6633.

LESSON 27—CREATING A RUBRIC FOR STUDENT-LED PARENT CONFERENCES

Objective

Students will review rubrics. Students will create a rubric for student-led parent conferences.

Preparation

Gather examples of rubrics and make transparencies. (See pp. 44–49.)

Content

1. Review the term rubric. (See p. 43.)
2. Give several examples.
3. Explain that the class will create a rubric for student-led parent conferences.
4. Brainstorm ideas for a successful student-led parent conference. (See the standard on p. 103.)
5. Put these ideas into a standard.
6. Develop the "novice," "emerging," and "exceeds standard" categories.

Post Preparation

Type the rubric for student-led parent conferences and have students place it behind the Visitor Log during the next scheduled portfolio time.

Rubric for Student-Led Parent Conferences

EXCEEDS STANDARD **EX**	I follow the conference agenda, and I check off each item as it is completed. I make appropriate introductions. I answer parent questions with thoughtful answers. I give a full explanation for each agenda item. I write two or more goals with my parent.
STANDARD **ST**	I follow the conference agenda. I make appropriate introductions. I answer parent questions satisfactorily. I briefly explain each agenda item. I write one goal with my parent.
EMERGING **EM**	I follow the agenda some of the time. I make introductions with help. I am unsure of answers for parent questions. I explain about half of the agenda items. My parent writes the goal for me without my help.
NOVICE **NO**	I am not sure how to follow the agenda. I make introductions with help and reminders. I need help to answer parent questions. I explain one or two of the agenda items. I do not write goals.

From *Practical Portfolios*. ©1994. Teacher Ideas Press, P.O. Box 6633, Englewood, CO 80155-6633.

LESSON 28—FALL CONFERENCE AGENDA REHEARSAL

Objective

Students will role-play the conference agenda.

Preparation

Prepare the Conference Confirmation Letter to give parents advance notice of their scheduled conference time. (See sample on p. 105.)

Content

1. Briefly review conference agenda items 2–12 (see p. 101) with the class. Item 1 concerning introductions will be practiced in Lesson 30.
2. Assign partners.
3. Have students alternate the roles of parent and student. At this time, students rehearse only agenda items 2–12. Have each student sign their partner's Visitor Log after the conference practice.
4. Explain the letter to parents with confirmation of conference times.

Date_____

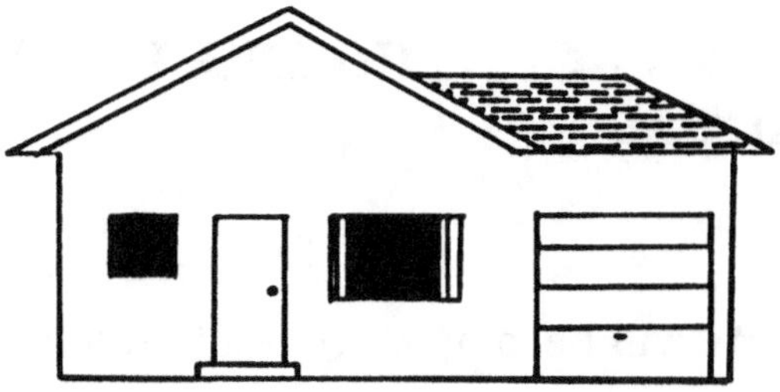

Dear Parents,

I appreciate the positive response to our planning for student-led parent conferences. This is to confirm your time for the conference with your child from _____ to _____ on _____. If you volunteered to provide cookies, please plan to send them with your child on the morning of the conferences.

You will receive an invitation from your student as a reminder several days before the conference, but I wanted to give you this advance notice also.

I look forward to seeing you.

Sincerely,

106 / 5—Fall Student-Led Parent Conferences

LESSON 29—CONTINUING THE FALL CONFERENCE AGENDA REHEARSAL

Objective

Students will become more familiar with their own explanations of agenda items 2–12.

Content

1. If necessary, review the conference agenda.
2. Assign different partners for this rehearsal.
3. Practice agenda items 2–12. Have each student sign their partner's Visitor Log after the conference practice.

LESSON 30—PRACTICING THE COMPLETE AGENDA

Objective

Students will make appropriate introductions and understand the complete conference agenda.

Preparation

1. Plan room setup. (See example on p. 107.)
2. Duplicate the Parent Evaluation form. (See p. 108.)

Content

1. Teach the steps of parent-teacher introductions.
2. Have two students role-play introductions.
3. Explain the room setup for the evening, walking through the various locations from room entry to serving of refreshments.
4. Explain the Parent Evaluation forms and where they will be located during conferences.
5. Have students choose partners.
6. Have two students demonstrate introductions in item 1. Have one of the students move to the correct locations in the room to show the placement of writing paper for the parent letter, refreshments, and the Parent Evaluation form in item 10.
7. Have all students role-play the total agenda, signing the Visitor Log of their partner.
8. Plan additional rehearsals as needed.

Lesson 30—Practicing the Complete Agenda / 107

FRONT CHALKBOARD

OUTSIDE DOOR

```
┌─────────────────────────────┐
│        EVALUATIONS          │
│       WRITING PAPER         │
│    SAMPLE LIFE SKILLS GOALS │
└─────────────────────────────┘
```

3:00 P.M. Amy
4 Sam
5 Jon   TABLE 2
6 Jason
7 Beth
8 Angela

3:00 P.M. Laurie
4 Mark
5 Emily   TABLE 3
6 Michelle
7 Jeff
8

REFRESHMENTS

3:00 P.M.
4
5 Mara   TABLE 4
6 Tammy
7 Brian
8

3:00 P.M. Jessica
4 Monica
5 Tim   TABLE 1
6 Adam
7 Brad
8 Janell

3:00 P.M. Erika
4 Devon
5 Jennifer   TABLE 5
6 Marc
7 Andrea
8 Tonja

Additional conference
sign-up sheet

TEACHER DESK

DOOR TO HALL

From *Practical Portfolios*. ©1994. Teacher Ideas Press, P.O. Box 6633, Englewood, CO 80155-6633.

Parent Evaluation of Fall Conferences

Please help evaluate our student-led parent conferences by completing this form. Thank you!

1. The time allowed for the student-led parent conference was (circle the answer)

   too little   about right   too much

2. Please rate how much the conference helped you understand your child's goals and current performance. (Circle the number.)

   a little   very much

   1   2   3   4   5

3. Please comment on the portfolio itself (arrangement, contents, changes you would like to see, etc.).

   _____
   _____
   _____
   _____

4. Please comment on any changes in the student-led parent conference you would suggest for next time.

   _____
   _____
   _____
   _____

5. Please comment on the format, which provides considerable time for a student-led parent conference but allows you to set up an additional private conference if you find it is desirable.

   _____
   _____
   _____
   _____

6. Please write any additional comments on the other side of this paper.

   Signature_____

LESSON 31—STUDENT INVITATIONS TO PARENTS

Objective

Students will make invitations for student-led parent conferences.

Preparation

1. Prepare a sample invitation and corresponding overhead transparency.
2. Prepare a list of final conference times for student information. Make an overhead transparency of conference times if desired.

Content

1. Give direct instruction on the basics of invitation writing, including who, what, when, where, and why.
2. Have students design and write an invitation to their parents.

Tips for Student-Led Parent Conferences

1. Decorations should be festive and bright, emphasizing the celebration theme of the evening.
2. Refreshments should be ready to serve as needed.
3. The teacher may find it easier to have the room parent organize the refreshments and decorations.
4. Post outside the room the schedule indicating each student's time and table number.
5. It may be helpful to display a poster reminding parents to be positive and to emphasize the successes of the student.
6. Be sure portfolios, journals, and any other necessary materials are ready and organized. Writing paper and pens should be available for parent letters to students. Sample Life Skills Goals and Parent Evaluations should be duplicated and placed on the table.
7. Arrange groups of desks to allow space between them.
8. Set out a sign-up sheet for parents to request an additional conference or phone call with the teacher if desired.
9. The teacher should circulate among the tables to observe the conferences and to be available to answer any questions. However, the child should remain in charge. If the teacher allows 1 hour for each set of conferences, there should be sufficient time to interact with parents.

LESSON 32—STUDENT THANK-YOU NOTES TO PARENTS

Objective

Students will practice correct letter form by writing thank-you notes to parents.

Content

1. Review the letter-writing form for the friendly letter.
2. Have students write thank-you notes.

LESSON 33—STUDENT EVALUATION OF FALL CONFERENCES AND PORTFOLIOS

Objective

Students will discuss feelings and reactions to the fall student-led parent conferences and portfolios. They will complete written evaluations.

Preparation

Duplicate the Student Fall Evaluation. (See p. 111.)

Content

1. Discuss students' feelings and reactions to the fall student-led parent conferences and portfolios.
2. Distribute and discuss the evaluation form. Encourage students to be honest and to think through answers carefully.
3. Have students complete the evaluation form.

Lesson 33—Student Evaluation of Fall Conferences and Portfolios / 111

Student Name _____ Date_____

Student Fall Evaluation

Your opinions are important! Please think carefully and give complete answers to the following:

1. Explain why you think we do student-led parent conferences.

2. Explain how you feel about student-led parent conferences and give some reasons for your feelings.

3. List some things that should stay the same the next time we do student-led parent conferences.

4. List some things that you would change the next time and how you would change them.

5. Do you have a better understanding of what you are doing in school because of portfolios and student-led parent conferences? Explain.

6. What do you think of your portfolio so far this year?

7. Is there anything you would like to change or add to the portfolio?

8. Please make any additional comments on the other side.

From *Practical Portfolios*. ©1994. Teacher Ideas Press, P.O. Box 6633, Englewood, CO 80155-6633.

6 Ongoing Portfolio Lessons

ONGOING PORTFOLIO LESSONS

During the first quarter of the school year, the lessons for the portfolio have been specific. These lessons have been geared toward assembling the portfolio and preparing it for the first student-led parent conferences. For the portfolio project to be successful, time should be scheduled each week throughout the year for ongoing portfolio activities. Examples of ongoing portfolio lessons are presented here.

Life Skills, Reading, Writing, and Math Sections

1. Have students review goals and fill out goal sheets for completed goals. Students need evidence that goals have been attained, such as work samples, a parent's signature, a teacher's signature, and so on. (See pp. 95-96.)

2. Have students write new goals as current goals are attained or as the need for other goals becomes apparent.

3. Confer with students on completed goals and the new goals that have been written. The teacher approves and dates the attained goals on the title pages.

4. Have students staple colored paper squares on their decorated name cards, which are displayed in the room. Each colored square represents an attained goal.

5. Have students color in 1 degree on the class thermometer for each attained goal.

6. By looking at the number of squares on the student name cards, you can see which students have not been completing goals. Schedule an extra conference with those students to discuss strategies toward goal attainment.

7. Discuss the selection of other items to be included in these sections. Have students choose papers of which they are especially proud. These do not necessarily have to be perfect papers. The papers may demonstrate mastery of new concepts, new strategies, or tasks completed well.

Life Skills

1. Have students continue writing Life Skills summaries each quarter.

2. Have students add any career awareness materials they have completed such as additional applications, job shadow experiences, and peer tutor evaluations.

3. Have students add other information as listed on the title page. (See p. 30.)

Writing

1. As writing evaluations are completed throughout the year, students place the self-adhesive labels on the summary section of the title page. (See p. 74.) These summaries provide foundations for demonstrating goal completion and for writing new goals.

2. Specifically at midyear, a second writing sample should be collected and evaluated. This should be completed before the portfolio goes home at the semester's end for a student-led parent conference.

3. Have students continue to add other writing samples as suggested on the title page. (See p. 32.)

Reading

1. Continue to write teacher summaries on the Reading title page, based upon teacher observations and notes taken during reader's workshop conferences. These continue to be the foundations for demonstrating goal completion and for writing new goals. This should be done at least quarterly.

2. Have students add samples of book projects.

Math

1. Have students continue writing Math summaries each quarter.
2. Have students update the district checklist of math skills.
3. Have students update their progress on the math facts graph.
4. Have students add samples of their math papers.

VIP

Have students continue to write about any important events as they occur throughout the year.

Science and Social Studies

Science and social studies activities may fit in several different areas. For example, consider a science activity that asks the students to calculate their weights on different planets. This activity could be placed in the Math section because of the calculations used or in the Life Skills section due to the critical thinking skills needed. Use your own discretion in deciding the placement of the assignment.

An interesting way to show completed projects that are too large for the portfolio is to take photos of them. Students can mount these pictures and explain the projects in writing.

LESSON 34—COMPLETING THE EXIT OUTCOME PAGE

Objective

Students will relate the class activities for the semester to the long-term goals of the student exit outcomes.

Note: Teachers may need to adjust this activity to match their own district's outcomes. Those whose districts have not yet written outcomes may choose to use the outcomes presented here or may disregard this lesson.

Preparation

1. Prepare an overhead transparency of the Exit Outcomes Semester Summary. (See p. 115.)
2. Prepare a list of activities performed during the semester for your own information.
3. Place the activities in the appropriate boxes on the Exit Outcomes Semester Summary for your own information. (See example on p. 116.)

Content

1. Brainstorm and record on the chalkboard all the activities, projects, and assignments that were completed during the semester.
2. Review the Student Exit Outcomes page with the students, including the meaning of each box. (See p. 39.)
3. Demonstrate how a few activities fit into the various boxes on the Exit Outcomes Semester Summary. Write these activities on the overhead transparency. Although most activities apply to more than one outcome, each activity is recorded in only one box.
4. Have students relate the remaining activities to the appropriate outcome box while you record these ideas on the transparency.

Post Preparation

From the transparency, type a copy of all generated ideas and duplicate this for the students. When convenient, have students place the completed page in their portfolios in front of the Student Exit Outcomes page from Lesson 4.

Lesson 34—Completing the Exit Outcome Page / 115

LOOK AT ALL WE DID WHILE WORKING
TOWARD OUR STUDENT EXIT OUTCOMES

The roles expected of the successful adult in the twenty-first century

EFFECTIVE COMMUNICATOR	QUALITY WORKER
SELF-DIRECTED LEARNER	COMPLEX THINKER
ETHICAL PERSON	RESPONSIBLE CITIZEN

THE FOUNDATION—Outcomes are built on a foundation of

BASIC SKILLS—*Reading*   *Writing*   *Math*

CULTURAL KNOWLEDGE

PERSONAL WELL-BEING

Credit to Jefferson County School District

From *Practical Portfolios.* ©1994. Teacher Ideas Press, P.O. Box 6633, Englewood, CO 80155-6633.

**LOOK AT ALL WE DID WHILE WORKING
TOWARDS OUR STUDENT EXIT OUTCOMES**

The roles expected of the successful adult in the twenty-first century

EFFECTIVE COMMUNICATOR Ben Franklin musical Poetry presentations Pie selling Fiction stories	QUALITY WORKER ITBS testing Biography projects Interviews Applications Ameritowne job training
SELF-DIRECTED LEARNER Student Attitude Measure Discovery D.A.R.E. program Earth Day pennants Reading and Writing Reflections Calendar/student planner Self-evaluation	COMPLEX THINKER Tar Wars posters Chemical demo "Imagine" journal Colonial houses Ameritowne money
ETHICAL PERSON Conflict mediation Young Ameritowne Hall of Life Lung Demo Class meetings Thank-you notes Campaign worker	RESPONSIBLE CITIZEN Growing and changing unit Student Leadership Foil collecting Class portfolio thermometer Pride in School Assembly Obeyed town laws at Ameritowne

THE FOUNDATION—Outcomes are built on a foundation of

BASIC SKILLS—*Reading* Bloom balls, Mystery mansions Smith reading strategies Biographies Janet Stephens, author assembly	*Writing* Reports Peer conferencing Autobiographies Rebus stories	*Math* STAMM clusters Problem solving Manipulatives

CULTURAL KNOWLEDGE
Colonial Days, candlemaking, art museum field trip, tin punching, butter making

PERSONAL WELL-BEING
Handbells, field day, choir, arts festival, mile run, crowded places, calorie burn, self-concept T-shirts, intramurals, 5th-grade musical, healthy-food party

From *Practical Portfolios*. ©1994. Teacher Ideas Press, P.O. Box 6633, Englewood, CO 80155-6633.

7 Sending the Portfolios Home: Midyear Student-Led Parent Conferences

LESSON 35—SENDING THE PORTFOLIOS HOME

Objective

Students will understand the procedures for taking portfolios home at midyear.

Preparation

1. Duplicate the letter home to parents. (See p. 118.)
2. Duplicate the Conference Agenda for students. (See p. 119.)
3. Before this lesson, students will have completed an Exit Outcome Semester Summary. (See p. 116.)

Content

1. Discuss with students the importance of sharing progress and work samples with parents between the fall and the spring student-led parent conferences.
2. Explain the parent letter that accompanies the portfolio home.
3. Read through the Conference Agenda with students.
4. Clarify the deadline for returning portfolios. To accommodate the schedules of today's busy families, a week is allowed for the portfolio at home.
5. Option: Have students practice the procedures with a partner as they did for the fall student-led parent conferences in chapter 5.

Date _____

Dear Parents,

Your student is bringing home the portfolio today. Some additions have been made, goals have been met, new goals have been written, and a semester summary relating to the district's exit outcomes has been completed by the class. I would appreciate it if you could set aside a special time of 10 to 20 minutes to look over the portfolio with your child, make comments, ask questions, and include any VIP information or goal writing.

*ALL PORTFOLIOS NEED TO BE RETURNED BY*_____

It would be wonderful if students could share the portfolio with other family members or others who might be interested. I have asked students to be sure to sit with anyone who looks at the portfolio and do their best to explain the different parts. All comments and signatures in the Visitor Log are welcome.

We have allowed one week for the portfolios to be home. Students may return them earlier if they have finished showing them. It is very important that care be taken with the portfolio to insure the safety of the contents. Much of it is irreplaceable. You will see the portfolio once again in May at the spring celebration of student success. More information on this will be sent later.

Please complete the brief questionnaire below to help us improve this activity in the future. Thank you for your help.

* *

Circle answer.

1. The length of time at home for the portfolio was

    too short   just about right   too long

2. My student was able to answer questions and explain the portfolio

    fairly well   about half the time   not very well

3. How many minutes were spent reviewing the portfolio?

    less than 10   10–20   more than 20

4. How many people reviewed the portfolio?_____

5. Was it worthwhile for the portfolio to come home at midyear?

    not very worthwhile   moderately worthwhile   very worthwhile

6. Should it come home more often?   yes   no

7. Other comments?_____

_____

Parent Signature: _____

From *Practical Portfolios*. ©1994. Teacher Ideas Press, P.O. Box 6633, Englewood, CO 80155-6633.

Midyear Student-Led Parent Conference Agenda

These guidelines are for a conference with your parents, who have already seen your portfolio once. If you are showing someone else, you need to follow most of the agenda that we used for our fall student-led parent conferences.

___1. Remind your audience that we are doing portfolios in order to 1) set goals and evaluate them; 2) collect various samples of work and organize them; and 3) better understand what we are learning and how it applies to our future goals.

___2. Take out the Visitor Log so that you remember to have visitors sign it at the end of the conference.

___3. Explain how we brainstormed all of our activities and then decided where to list them in our student exit outcomes.

___4. Review each section. Go over the summary and goals and explain how you think you are doing in each area. Ask your audience to make comments. You may write more goals together if you wish. Show any new papers you have added.

____Life Skills   ____Reading

____Writing   ____Math

___5. Try to brainstorm more ideas for the VIP section. Anything you are proud of should be written down, no matter how small it may seem. Having the courage to enter a contest is as important as winning one. Doing a special favor for someone, earning money by doing a responsible job, or getting a new pet for your birthday all belong in the VIP section. Include anything that is important to you in any way!

___6. Ask the visitors viewing your portfolio to sign the Visitor Log and make comments.

___7. Ask the visitors to complete the short questionnaire about the portfolios.

___8. Place both items in your portfolio and put it in a safe place to return to school.

From *Practical Portfolios*. ©1994. Teacher Ideas Press, P.O. Box 6633, Englewood, CO 80155-6633.

8 End-of-the-Year Portfolio Lessons

LESSON 36—END-OF-THE-YEAR WRITING SAMPLE

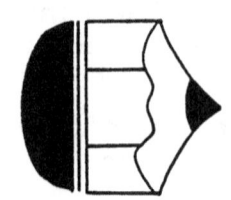

Objective

Students will compare and contrast the Creative Writing Checklists from the beginning and end of the year. They will graph their progress in writing.

Preparation

1. Evaluate a creative writing story for each child according to the Creative Writing Checklist.
2. Complete a Creative Writing Checklist for each student.
3. The overhead transparency of the checklist should be available.
4. The graph was placed in the portfolio before the first student-led parent conference.
5. Option: Have students evaluate themselves using a Creative Writing Checklist.

Content

1. Review Lesson 20, page 74, explaining the Creative Writing Checklist.
2. Instruct students to refer to their Creative Writing Checklist Graphs from the beginning of the year. They should note their demonstrated writing characteristics for each area.
3. Distribute the evaluated stories and the Creative Writing Checklists for the end of the year.
4. Have students decide on their best area and mark it with a star.
5. Have students choose the area they feel needs improvement and mark it with "needs work."
6. Have students record the results of the Creative Writing Checklist on the same graph used for the first writing sample, using a contrasting color.
7. Have students complete the Writing Sample Cover information for the end-of-the-year writing sample and place it in the portfolio, followed by the checklist and story.

LESSON 37—END-OF-THE-YEAR WRITING SURVEY

Objective

Students will complete a second Writing Survey. For instructions, see Lesson 15, p. 64.

In the next lesson, students will compare and contrast their surveys from the beginning and the end of the year.

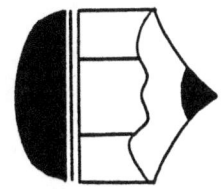

LESSON 38—WRITING SELF-REFLECTIONS

Objective

Students will compare and contrast the Writing Surveys from the beginning and the end of the year. Students will complete the Writing Reflections page.

Preparation

1. Duplicate the Writing Reflections page in the designated color. (See p. 122.)
2. Duplicate the Writing Strategies page. (See p. 123.) Do not three-hole punch this page because it is for reference only.

Content

1. Distribute completed end-of-the-year Writing Surveys. Have students turn, in the portfolio, to the Writing Survey from the beginning of the year.
2. Explain that the purpose of this activity is to find the similarities and differences in the two Writing Surveys.
3. Give some examples of how responses on the surveys may have changed or remained the same. Students may notice changes in attitudes toward writing, in the connection between reading and writing, and in the use of different writing strategies.
4. Allow students to compare and contrast their two surveys.
5. Distribute the Writing Reflections page.
6. Read and give examples for each question, giving students thinking and writing time.
7. To answer question no. 3 on the Writing Reflections page, have students use the Writing Strategies page.
8. When completed, have students place the Writing Reflections page and the Writing Survey in the portfolio at the end of the Writing section.

Name_____ Date_____

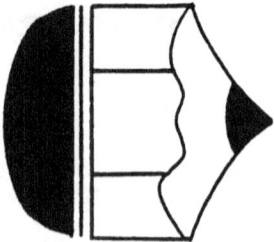

Writing Reflections

1. How have your opinions about writing changed since your first survey?

   a._____

   _____

   b._____

   _____

2. Do you think these changes are positive changes? Why or why not?

   _____

   _____

   _____

3. Tell something new you have learned in writing.

   _____

   _____

   _____

   _____

4. Complete the following statements: From my Creative Writing Checklist, I can tell I have improved on

   _____

   _____

   _____

   _____

5. Now I would like to concentrate on improving

   _____

   _____

   _____

   _____

From *Practical Portfolios*. ©1994. Teacher Ideas Press, P.O. Box 6633, Englewood, CO 80155-6633.

Writing Strategies

1. I write only on one side of the paper so I can cut and paste to revise.
2. I skip lines in order to insert words and phrases later.
3. I don't erase because I may want to use a previous idea.
4. I show through description rather than telling. For example, instead of writing that someone looks angry, I describe the furrowed brows, the blazing eyes, and the rough tone of voice of that person.
5. I confer for meaning with my classmates. What does the reader need to know and understand?
6. I proofread for spelling and punctuation after the meaning is the way I want it.
7. I don't throw away stories or parts of stories. I may revise later or use the idea in another story.
8. I brainstorm to get ideas for my writing.
9. I use mapping to develop an idea.
10. I use a storyline worksheet for development of plot.
11. I notice what good writers do. For example, I notice how they begin and end stories, describe settings, and develop characters.
12. When I proofread, I read through my paper several times, reading for meaning, word choice, punctuation, spelling, and handwriting.
13. I record writing ideas as I think of them to refer to later.

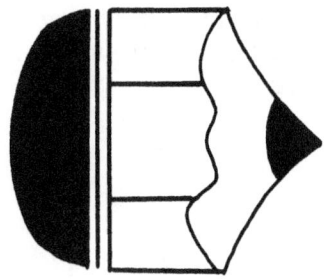

LESSON 39—END-OF-THE-YEAR READING SURVEY

Objective

Students will complete a second Reading Survey.

Preparation

For instructions see Lesson 14, page 62.

In Lesson 41, students will compare and contrast their surveys from the beginning and the end of the year.

LESSON 40—ADDING JOURNAL ENTRIES AND READING LOGS TO THE PORTFOLIOS

Objective

Students select two reading journal entries, one from the beginning and one from the end of the year, to be used in the portfolio for comparison and demonstration of growth in journal writing. Students place the Reading Log (list of books read during the year) in the portfolio.

Content

1. Have each student select a journal entry representative of writing at the beginning of the year.

2. Have each student select a journal entry representative of writing at the end of the year.

3. Have students compare the two samples. They may notice changes in clarity, description, detail, punctuation, handwriting, and so on. The samples are placed in the portfolio at the end of the Reading section.

4. Have students place their Reading Logs in the same section of the portfolio.

LESSON 41—READING SELF-REFLECTIONS

Objective

The students will compare and contrast the Reading Surveys from the beginning and end of the year. Students will complete the Reading Reflections page.

Preparation

1. Duplicate the Reading Reflections page in the designated color. (See p. 126.)
2. Duplicate the Reading Strategies page. (See p. 127.) It is for reference only and does not need to be three-hole punched.

Content

1. Distribute completed end-of-the-year Reading Surveys. Have students turn, in the portfolio, to the Reading Survey from the beginning of the year.
2. Explain that the purpose of this activity is to find the similarities and differences in the Reading Surveys from the beginning and end of the year.
3. Give some examples of how the responses on the surveys may have changed or remained the same. For example, students may notice changes in attitudes about reading, in the types of books read, and in the authors preferred.
4. Allow students to compare and contrast their two surveys.
5. Distribute the Reading Reflections page.
6. Read and give examples for each question, giving students thinking and writing time.
7. To answer question no. 3 on the Reading Reflections page, have students use the Reading Strategies page.
8. Have students place the completed Reading Reflections page and Reading Survey in their portfolios at the end of the Reading section.

Name_____ Date_____

Reading Reflections

1. How have your opinions about reading changed since your first survey?

   a._____
   _____

   b._____
   _____

2. Do you think these changes are positive changes? Why or why not?
   _____
   _____
   _____
   _____

3. Tell something new you have learned in reading.
   _____
   _____
   _____
   _____

4. How have your reading journal entries changed since the beginning of the year?
   _____
   _____
   _____
   _____

5. Complete the following statement: I would like to concentrate on improving
   _____
   _____
   _____
   _____

From *Practical Portfolios*. ©1994. Teacher Ideas Press, P.O. Box 6633, Englewood, CO 80155-6633.

Reading Strategies

1. The more I know about a book, the easier it is to read. I use what I already know to help me read.
2. I read directly for meaning. If I make a mistake that does not affect meaning, I don't go back to correct myself.
3. I preview pictures, headings, and charts. I form questions from previewing.
4. I keep reading, and I don't slow down.
5. I use the following strategies for new words:
    a. I skip some words I don't know, using context to help clarify as I read.
    b. I make logical guesses. I read past the unknown words and go back.
    c. I ask someone the word if I don't know it.
    d. I sound out the word.
6. I learn to be a better reader by reading.
7. I study charts before looking at the questions. I look at key labels, colors, and titles.
8. When reading a short passage with questions, I read the questions first.
9. I skim and scan when looking for specific information.
10. I look for key words. I circle, underline, or highlight them if possible.

From *Practical Portfolios*. ©1994. Teacher Ideas Press, P.O. Box 6633, Englewood, CO 80155-6633.

LESSON 42—MISCELLANEOUS ACTIVITIES

Objective

Students will complete a Math Skills Demonstration page and an end-of-the-year computer sample and place a photocopy of one page from the book they are currently reading into the portfolio.

Note: These activities should be completed at different times rather than all in the same period.

Preparation

1. Duplicate copies of the Math Skills Demonstration page on page 67.
2. Have students choose and print their best computer project of the year.
3. Collect current reading books and make photocopies of one page from each student's book.

Content

1. Follow directions for the Math Skills Demonstration page on page 66.
2. Follow directions for the computer skills demonstration on page 68.
3. Distribute photocopies of reading book pages to students. Have them record the date at the top, three-hole punch the pages, and place them in the Reading section of the portfolio behind the fall photocopy.
4. Have students compare fall and spring samples of the above activities for demonstrated growth. This comparison could be done with a partner.

9 Spring Student-Led Parent Conferences

LESSON 43—SPRING STUDENT-LED PARENT CONFERENCES

Objective

Students will review the purpose of student-led parent conferences.

Preparation

Duplicate the parent letter. (See pp. 130-31.)
Duplicate the Home Responsibility Inventory. (See p. 27.)

Content

1. Review the purpose of the student-led parent conferences as expressed in the parent letter.
2. Students review the Rubric for Student-Led Parent Conferences. (See p. 103.) Each student placed a copy of this rubric behind the Visitor Log before the fall conferences.
3. When inventories are returned, place them in the Life Skills section.

LESSON 44—COMPLETION OF EXIT OUTCOME PAGE FOR SECOND SEMESTER

Objective

Students will relate second-semester class activities to the district's student exit outcomes.

Preparation

See Lesson 34, page 114, for the lesson instructions.

Date_____

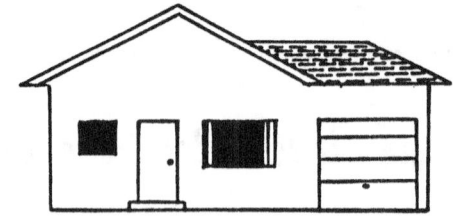

SPRING STUDENT-LED PARENT CONFERENCES

Dear Parents,

Our spring student-led parent conferences will be on _____ from _____to_____. This is an opportunity for you, as a parent, to display a positive interest in your child's progress, accept your child's evaluation of accomplishments, and provide your child with support and encouragement for work done at school. Student goals include the following:

1. Being responsible for reporting school achievements.
2. Learning to communicate.
3. Learning to evaluate their work honestly and fairly.
4. Becoming accountable for work and behavior.
5. Learning organizational and leadership skills.

Five to seven conferences of 30 to 40 minutes each will be taking place at one time. I will be in the room, acting as a facilitator and available for clarification, if necessary. I would like to stress that your child is conducting the conference, and we must honor this role.

A few hints for a successful conference:

1. Be positive. Put the emphasis on what your child does well. Whatever we give attention to grows and flourishes, and this certainly applies to our children's feelings of accomplishment and self-esteem.
2. Know that you will see a finished piece of writing and some rough drafts. This is not a time to point out missing punctuation and spelling errors; rather, concentrate on the content of the writing.
3. Discuss the goals that your child has written and achieved.
4. Before the conference is over, please write a note expressing your appreciation of your child.
5. Enjoy refreshments and complete an evaluation of your conference. I welcome any suggestions for improvement.

Please indicate on the following page your first and second time choices for your celebration with your child, and if you can contribute refreshments. Also, complete the attached Home Responsibility Inventory to be returned with your time choices. I am looking forward to seeing you at our celebration of success. Thank you for your support!

Sincerely,

Lesson 44—Completion of Exit Outcome Page for Second Semester / 131

DETACH AND RETURN THIS PAGE BY _____

Please indicate if you can contribute a dozen cookies. Send them to school on the morning of _____

_____ Yes, I will contribute one dozen cookies for the celebration.

_____ PARENT SIGNATURE

PLEASE MARK YOUR FIRST AND SECOND CHOICES FOR TIMES BELOW.
If you can come at any time, check on the appropriate line.

TIME	FIRST CHOICE	SECOND CHOICE
_____	_____	_____
_____	_____	_____
_____	_____	_____
_____	_____	_____
_____	_____	
ANYTIME	_____	

COMMENTS:_____

_____

_____

_____

From *Practical Portfolios.* ©1994. Teacher Ideas Press, P.O. Box 6633, Englewood, CO 80155-6633.

LESSON 45—INTRODUCTION TO THE SPRING CONFERENCE AGENDA

Objective

Students will become familiar with the spring conference agenda.

Preparation

1. Duplicate the conference agenda. (See p. 133.)
2. Plan the conference schedule after requests for time slots are returned.

Content

1. Read through agenda items 1–6 and 8 as each student turns to the corresponding page in the portfolio.
2. Have students rehearse silently how they would explain each agenda item to their parents.
3. Explain that demonstration items will be added and rehearsed later.

Lesson 45—Introduction to the Spring Conference Agenda / 133

SPRING STUDENT-LED PARENT CONFERENCE AGENDA

___ 1. Get your portfolio and go to your assigned table.

___ 2. Remove the Visitor Log so that you remember to ask for a signature and comments at the end of your conference.

___ 3. Explain how we brainstormed all of our activities for this semester and decided how they applied to the student exit outcomes.

___ 4. Life Skills
Compare for growth the fall and the spring Home Responsibility Inventories.
Show and explain your computer project.
Review goals in general and talk about where you have improved.

___ 5. Reading
Review your goals.
Retell the story and read a paragraph from your photocopy.
Read your Reading Reflections page.
Show your best reading journal entry and your Reading Log.

___ 6. Writing
Read your last story.
Discuss the teacher comments for the story.
Read your goals.
Compare the two Creative Writing Checklists.
Read your Writing Reflections page.

___ 7. Math
Review your goals.
Explain the Math Skills Demonstration page and compare it with the one in the fall.
Demonstrate a math concept using this manipulative:_____

___ 8. VIP
Explain anything you have included here and add any items you wish.

___ 9. Science
Demonstrate this activity:_____

___10. Social Studies
Explain this activity:_____

___11. Parents: Write a short letter to your child expressing positives. Place it in the Life Skills section of the portfolio. During this time, students may get refreshments and an evaluation.

___12. Have your parents sign the Visitor Log. Turn in the evaluation of the conference. Thank your parents for coming.

___13. Clean up your table and put your portfolio away.

From *Practical Portfolios*. ©1994. Teacher Ideas Press, P.O. Box 6633, Englewood, CO 80155-6633.

LESSON 46—CHOOSING A MATH MANIPULATIVE

Objective

Students will select one math manipulative to demonstrate at student-led parent conferences.

Preparation

Prepare a list of math manipulatives used this year to serve as a reference.

Content

1. Brainstorm the math manipulatives used during the year that the students would like to show their parents on conference night.

2. Have students select by vote three or four different manipulatives to present.

3. Have each student select one of the manipulatives and write the choice in the appropriate space on the conference agenda. (The number of activities from which students may choose is up to the teacher's discretion. However, due to the time and space involved in setting up a number of different activities, it is helpful to limit the number of student choices.)

4. Record the number of students who will be doing each activity so the necessary materials can be available.

LESSON 47—SELECTING SCIENCE AND SOCIAL STUDIES ACTIVITIES

Objective

Students will select one science activity and one social studies activity to demonstrate at student-led parent conferences.

Preparation

Prepare lists of science and social studies activities completed this year to use as a reference.

Content

1. Brainstorm the science and social studies activities completed during the year for students to show their parents on conference night.
2. Have students select by vote three or four different activities for each subject to present.
3. Have each student select a science activity and a social studies activity and write the choices in the appropriate places on the conference agenda. (As noted in the math manipulative lesson, it is helpful to limit the number of student choices.)
4. Record the number of students who are doing each activity so the necessary materials can be prepared.

LESSON 48—SPRING CONFERENCE AGENDA REHEARSAL

Objective

Students will role-play the Spring Conference Agenda.
Note: Student will again prepare invitations and write thank-you notes for conferences as in the fall. (See Lessons 31 and 32.)

Preparation

1. Prepare materials for math, science, and social studies activities.
2. Sometime before this lesson, meet with the groups about the specific activities. Review procedures and give examples of presentations.
3. Plan the room setup and duplicate the Parent Evaluation. (See p. 136.)
4. Prepare the Conference Confirmation Letter with students to give parents advance notice. (See p. 105.)

Content

1. If necessary, review the agenda.
2. Explain the location for the demonstration materials.
3. Assign partners and practice the entire agenda.
4. Explain the letter to parents with confirmation of conference times.

Spring Parent Evaluation

Please help us evaluate our spring student-led parent conferences and the portfolios by completing this form. Thank you!

1. The time allowed for the student-led parent conference was (circle answer)

    too little   about right   too much

2. Please rate how much the conference enabled you to understand your child's progress and activities. (Circle number.)

    not at all   very much
    1   2   3   4   5

3. Please comment on the portfolio itself, such as its arrangement, contents, changes you would like to see, and so on.

    _____
    _____
    _____
    _____

4. Please comment on the format of our fall student-led parent conference, a home mini-conference with the portfolio in January, and a spring student-led parent conference.

    too much   about right   not enough

5. Please comment on any changes in the student-led parent conference that you would suggest for next year.

    _____
    _____
    _____
    _____
    _____

6. Please make additional comments on the other side.

SIGNATURE_____

From *Practical Portfolios*. ©1994. Teacher Ideas Press, P.O. Box 6633, Englewood, CO 80155-6633.

LESSON 49—STUDENT EVALUATION OF SPRING CONFERENCES AND PORTFOLIOS

Objective

Students will discuss feelings and reactions to the spring student-led parent conferences and portfolios. They will complete written evaluations.

Preparation

Duplicate the Student Spring Evaluation. (See pp. 138-39.)

Content

1. Discuss students' feelings and reactions to the spring student-led parent conferences and portfolios.
2. Distribute and discuss the evaluation form. Encourage students to be honest and to think carefully about their answers.
3. Have students complete the evaluation form.

Post Preparation

For a discussion of what to do with portfolios at the end of the year, see page 10.

Student Name_____ Date_____

Student Spring Evaluation

Your opinions are important! Please think carefully and give complete answers.

1. Explain why you think we conduct student-led parent conferences.

2. Explain how you feel about student-led parent conferences and give some reasons for your feelings.

3. List some things you think should stay the same for student-led parent conferences.

4. List some things that should be changed and how you would change them.

5. Do you have a better understanding of what you are doing in school because of portfolios and student-led parent conferences? Explain your answer.

6. How would you rate your portfolio this year?
    Fair   OK   Outstanding   Awesome

7. Is there anything you would like to change in the way we did portfolios this year?

8. Is there anything you would like to add to the portfolios?

9. Check any of these statements that are true for you.

   _____I am surprised at how much I accomplished this year.

   _____I am disappointed I did not reach all of my goals.

   _____I am proud of myself.

   _____I want to continue working on my goals that I have written.

   _____Portfolios are not very important.

   _____Portfolios are fun.

   _____I hope I can do a portfolio next year.

   _____I think I work harder when I write my own goals.

   _____I like seeing my work from the school year in one collection.

10. My favorite part of portfolios and student-led parent conferences was

11. Other comments:

References

Atwell, Nancie. 1987. *In the middle: Writing, reading, and learning with adolescents.* Portsmouth, NH: Boynton/Cook.

Carbo, Marie, Rita Dunn, and Kenneth Dunn. 1986. *Teaching students to read through their individual learning styles.* Englewood Cliffs, NJ: Prentice-Hall.

Dawson, Vera. n.d. Using the tools of standards-based education to redefine the students' learning experience. Jefferson County Public School District R-1, Golden, CO. Photocopy.

Dismuke, Diane. 1993. Are report cards obsolete? *NEA Today* 11:12–13.

Enoki, Donald Y. 1992. *Student portfolios and profiles: A holistic approach to multiple assessment in whole language classrooms.* Paper presented at the annual meeting of the American Educational Research Association, San Francisco.

Finn, Chester E. 1991. *We must take charge: Our schools and our future.* New York: Free Press.

Gardner, Howard. 1983. *Frames of mind: The theory of multiple intelligences.* New York: Basic Books.

Hamburg, Beatrix A. 1990. *Life skills training: Preventive interventions for young adolescents.* Report of the life skills training working group, U.S. Congress Office of Technology Assessment's Adolescent Health Project, Washington, D.C. ERIC document number ED 323018.

Harrison School District 2. 1992. *Portfolio handbook—revised.* Colorado Springs, CO.

Hearne, Jill, and Steven Schuman. 1992. *Portfolio assessment: Implementation and use at an elementary level.* Technical Report, Washington State. ERIC document number ED 349330.

Hieronymus, A. N., H. D. Hoover, E. F. Lindquist, Kathleen R. Oberley, Nancy K. Cantor, Susan S. Eberly, Debbie D. Burbick, Gayle B. Bray, Linda J. Schuchert, Jan C. Lewis, Steve Rattenborg, Elizabeth L. Hyde, Audrey L. Qualls-Payne, David J. Martin, and Deborah L. Green. 1986. *Iowa tests of basic skills: Teacher's guide.* University of Iowa. Chicago: Riverside.

Jefferson County School District R-l. n.d. Creative Writing Criteria Checklist. Golden, CO. Photocopy.

———. School Effectiveness Unit. 1992. *Student outcomes and proficiencies.* Golden, CO. Pamphlet.

Little, Nancy, and John Allan. 1988. *Student-led teacher-parent conferences.* Toronto: Lugus Productions.

Rhodes, Lynn K., and Nancy Shanklin. 1993. *Windows into literacy: Assessing learners K–8*. Portsmouth, NH: Heinemann Press.

Romer, Roy. 1992. Standards and Reform. *American School Board Journal* 178 (9): 36–37.

Smith, Frank. 1985. *Reading without nonsense*. 2d ed. New York: Teachers College Press.

Taylor, Patty. 1991. *In the process: A visual arts portfolio assessment pilot project*. Descriptive report, California Art Education Association, Carmichael, CA. ERIC document number ED 323018.

Thornburg, David D. 1989. Learning curve: Multiple intelligences, a challenge for educational technology. *A+ Magazine* (February): 91–92.

Tierney, Robert, Mark A. Carter, and Laura E. Desai. 1991. *Portfolio assessment in the reading-writing classroom*. Norwood, MA: Christopher-Gordon.

Valencia, Sheila. 1990. A portfolio approach to classroom reading assessment: The whys, whats, and hows. *The Reading Teacher* 43: 338–40.

Vandamme, Kathy. 1992. Reading and Writing Standards. Jefferson County School District R-1, Golden, CO. Photocopy.

Wack, Bob, and Effective Learning Resources. n.d. *Motivating the unmotivated: Teaching self-motivation, self-discipline & responsibility*. Oakland, CA.

Weber, Richard A. 1993. "Thinking about standards in an era of reform and restructuring." Speech given in Arvada, Colorado.

Young Americans Education Foundation. 1989. *Young Ameritowne: A "hands-on" lesson in free enterprise*. Young Americans Education Foundation. Denver, CO.

Index

Academic concerns. *See* Parent concerns
Administrators, 4, 13, 14, 29
Advance preparations. *See* Portfolios
Agenda, 7, 11, 16, 17, 18, 132. *See also* Reproducibles; Student-led parent conferences
Allan, J., 7, 11
Anecdotal records, teacher, 31, 32
Anxiety, teacher and student, 15, 100
Application. *See* Life skills
Art, 8, 35, 36, 37, 38, 49, 71, 116
Assembling the portfolio. *See* Portfolio
Assessment, 13. *See also* Tests
   traditional, 1, 2, 12
   portfolio, 2, 3, 4, 9
      as assessment tools, 2, 12
      performance-based, 2, 7
      real-life validity, 5
Attitudes. *See* Student attitudes
Atwell, N., 9
Authentic reading, 2
Authentic tasks, 1, 12, 21–25. *See also* Life skills
Autobiographical writing, 30. *See also* Letter writing

Back-to-School Night, 20, 26
Bar graphs, 8, 10, 33, 74, 75, 120. *See also* Reproducibles
Basic skills, 1, 37
Behavior concerns. *See* Parent concerns
Behavior expectations, 9, 11, 43, 50. *See also* Goals; Rubrics; Reproducibles
Bodily/kinesthetic intelligence, 4, 5, 57. *See also* Seven Intelligences

Carbo, M., 57
Career awareness, 30, 112
Carter, M., 1, 2, 4
Celebrations, 11, 15, 35, 71, 98
Check writing. *See* Life skills
Checklist, 3, 9, 10, 12, 31, 32, 33, 113. *See also* Creative Writing Checklist; Reproducibles
Collaboration, between student, parent, teacher, 14, 21–25
Colorado, 6
Colorado Springs, Colorado, 6
Communication, 4, 7, 8, 11, 12, 13, 14, 37, 47, 98. *See also* Parent letter; Home responsibility inventory

Community, student involvement in, 88
Community in the classroom, building a, 16, 53
Complex thinker, 36, 37. *See also* Critical thinking skills
Composing goals. *See* Goals
Computer literacy, 9, 70, 88, 93
Computer skills sample, 10, 30, 68, 128
Conferences, 4, 84, 116. *See also* Student-led parent conferences; Reproducibles
   for goal attainment, 12, 17, 18
   notes of, 31, 32
   traditional conferences, 7, 11, 14, 26, 108, 109
Confidence. *See* Self-confidence
Conflict mediator, 58
Contests, 35, 70, 71
Cooperative learning, 9, 30, 42, 44, 50, 93. *See also* Reproducibles
   definition of, 41
Covers for portfolios. *See* Portfolios; Reproducibles
Creative Writing Checklist, 3, 9, 10, 74, 120. *See also* Reproducibles
Critical thinking skills, 4, 9, 14, 30
Cultural knowledge, 30, 37, 116

Dawson, V., 6
Decorations. *See* Student-led parent conferences
Departmentalized, 14
Desai, L., 1, 2, 4
Dismuke, D., 7
Drama, 58
Dunn, K., 57
Dunn, R., 57

Education 2000, 6
Effective communicator, 36, 37
Emerging. *See* Rubrics
End of the year portfolio lessons, 10, 120
End of the year portfolio plans, 10, 13, 17, 18
Enoki, D., 1, 2, 3
Ethical person, 37
Evaluation, 3, 4, 10, 15. *See also* Reproducibles; Student-led parent conferences: Student evaluations, Parent evaluations
   as part of instruction, 3

Example pages for teachers
  completed self-monitoring page, 51
  completed student exit outcomes semester summary, 116
  completed student goal writing for reading, 85
  completed student goal writing for writing, 86
  completed student summary and goal writing for life skills, 89
  completed student summary and goal writing for math, 91
  completed teacher summary for reading, 85
  completed teacher summary for writing, 86
  completed VIP student comments, 71
  room set up for conferences, 107
  student exit outcomes, 37
  student exit outcomes with illustrations, 39
Exceeds standards. See Rubrics
Exit outcomes. See Student exit outcomes; Reproducibles
Extracurricular activities, 5, 8. See also VIP

Final considerations, 12
Finn, C., 2
First of the year lessons, 9, 40

Gardner, H., 4, 5
Goals, 8, 11, 12, 13, 14, 15, 16, 17, 74, 82, 86, 89, 90. See also Reproducibles; Example pages for teachers: Completed student goal writing
  achievement, 3, 9, 10, 11
  attainment of, 10, 11, 13, 16, 17, 19, 50, 95, 96, 112, 113
  composing
    behavior, 92
    life skills, 9, 10, 89, 92, 93
    math, 10, 91, 92, 94
    reading, 10, 82, 85
    writing, 10, 73, 82, 86
  reaching your, 95, 96
  realistic, 3, 26, 50, 74
  setting, 13, 77
  statements, 10, 83, 84
Grades, 13
Graphs. See Bar graphs

Hamburg, B., 5
Hands-on activities, 18. See also Math manipulatives; Science; Social studies
Handwriting, 32, 59, 70, 84
Harrison School District, 6, 13
Harvard University, 4
Health, physical/mental, 30, 37
Hearne, J., 6
Heironymus, A., 1
Heritage, cultural and ethnic, 37
Hobbies, 40, 63

Home activities, 5, 88. See also VIP
Home responsibility inventory, 9, 20, 27, 30, 69, 87, 129, 130. See also Life skills
How to use this book, 7–12

Idea pages, 8, 88, 90
Illinois, 2
Illustrations, of exit outcomes by students, 9, 38, 39. See also Visual representations
Intelligence, 12. See also Seven intelligences
  measure of, 5
  study of, 4
Interests. See Student interests
Interviews. See Life skills
Introductions. See Student-led parent conferences: Introductions, during
Inventories for home. See Reproducibles
Invitations, 3, 32. See Student-led parent conferences
Iowa Test of Basic Skills, 1, 116
  uses for, 1

Jefferson County School District, 3, 6, 9, 37, 39, 78, 79
Job market, future, 6
Job shadow, 30, 88, 112
Journal entries, 2, 11, 16, 31, 33, 83, 124, 126. See also Reading: Journal

Kansas, 7
Kinesthetic learner, 57. See also Learning styles

Learning strategies. See Strategies, learning
Learning styles, 9, 30, 88, 93
  definition of, 57
Letter writing, 2, 32
  autobiographical letter, 9, 40
  friendly letter, 12, 40, 110
  thank you letters/notes, 7, 16, 17, 18, 110, 116, 135
Life skills, 5, 8, 9, 11, 12, 14, 15, 17, 27, 87, 88, 89, 90, 92, 93, 112. See also Example pages for teachers; Reproducibles; Summaries
  acquisition of new knowledge, 57
  applications, 6, 9, 30, 32, 50, 56, 58, 59, 60, 116
  checkwriting, 32, 58
  computer skills, 68
  definition of, 5
  home responsibility inventory, 69
  interviews, 6, 9, 12, 30, 60, 61, 70, 116
  problem solving, 67
  résumé writing, 61
  self-monitoring, 50
Lifelong learners, 1. See also Life skills

Listening, 37, 41, 46, 48, 88
Literature, 37, 83
Little, N., 7, 11
Linguistic intelligence, 4. *See also* Seven intelligences
Logical/Mathematical intelligence, 4. *See also* Seven intelligences

Math, 1, 3, 7, 8, 12, 14, 17, 33, 37, 87, 90, 91, 92, 94, 112, 113
   checklists, 12
   exit outcomes, and, 37
   goals, 92, 94
   idea page, 90
   problem-solving strategies, 3
   summaries, 87
   summary example, 91
Math, functional records, 33
Math manipulatives, 11, 94, 116, 134
Math skills demonstrations, 9, 10, 33, 66, 67, 87, 128. *See also* Reproducibles
Mathematical intelligence, 4. *See also* Seven intelligences
Maughmer, B., 7
Michigan, 2
Mini-lessons, 3, 9, 10
Miscellaneous activities, 16, 128
Music, 4, 14, 35, 71, 116
Musical intelligence, 4. *See also* Seven intelligences

Norm-referencing, 1
Norm-referenced tests, 1
   limitations of, 1–2
   uses for, 1
North America, 6
Novice. *See* Rubrics

Ongoing portfolio assessment, 3, 9, 26
Ongoing portfolio lessons, 10, 16, 17, 112, 113
Organizing work into the portfolio. *See* Portfolios
Outcome-based education, 6, 9, 12, 13, 14. *See also* Student exit outcomes

Parent concerns,
   academic, 11, 13, 15
   behavioral, 11, 15
Parent, duties of room volunteer, 12, 15, 60, 109
Parent education, 13
Parent involvement, 4, 7, 9, 11, 12, 13, 14, 26, 29, 63
Parent letter, 8, 11, 13, 14, 16, 17, 19, 20, 97, 98, 104, 105, 106, 118, 130–31. *See also* Reproducibles
Peer tutoring, 30, 58, 70
Performance-based assessment. *See* Assessment

Personal intelligences, 4, 5. *See also* Seven intelligences
   interpersonal, 4, 5
   intrapersonal, 4, 5
Physical education. *See* VIP, Health
Photocopy. *See* Reading
Portfolios, 2, 3, 4, 6, 26. *See also* Assessment; End of the year plan; End of the year portfolio lessons; Reproducibles; Rubrics; Title pages for portfolio sections
   advance preparations for, 16, 17, 19
   assembling the portfolio, 9, 16, 17, 28
   benefits of, 4
   components of, 8–9
   concept of, 2, 13, 16, 17, 20
   covers, 8, 9, 20, 28
   dividers, 9, 28
   evaluation of, 111, 137–39
   expectations, 9
   explaining to parents/administrators, 13, 20, 98
   illustrations of, 28
   introduction of, 20
   notebook, 3, 8, 9, 28
      description of, 19
   ongoing nature of, 15
   organizing work into, 9, 16, 17, 69
   overview of portfolio lessons, 9–10
   questions about, 13
   relationship to outcome-based education, 13
   room setup, 19
   scheduling weekly time for, 15, 20, 57
Problem solving, 3, 33, 37, 67, 116
Process instruction, 6. *See also* Process-oriented classrooms
Process learning, 1. *See also* Process-oriented classrooms
Process-oriented classrooms, 2, 7

Quality worker, 37

Reading, 1, 2, 4, 7–11, 14, 16, 27, 37, 46, 65, 69, 83, 112, 113. *See also* Journal entries; Reproducibles; Strategies
   comprehension, 1, 8, 45
   journal, 2, 11, 101, 124, 126
   logs, 16
      definition of, 124
   photocopy of page, 10, 31, 69, 128
   process, 2, 31
   reflections, 31, 125, 126
   survey, 9, 10, 31, 62, 63, 124
   workshop, 7, 8, 10, 113
Real-life tasks, 5, 41. *See also* Authentic tasks; Life skills

Reflections, 3, 10, 12, 16, 17, 53, 73, 87, 121, 125. *See also* Reading; Writing
Refreshments. *See* Student-led parent conferences
Regular parent teacher conferences. *See* Traditional parent conferences
Rehearsals. *See* Student-led parent conferences
Reports, 2
Reproducibles, 8
  agendas for student-led parent conference
    for fall, 101
    for midyear, 119
    for spring, 133
  application, 59
  bar graph for creative writing checklist, 80–81
  cooperative learning, 42
  creative writing checklist, 78–79
  exit outcomes semester summary page, 115
  evaluations
    by parent, 108, 118, 136
    by student, 111, 138
  goals
    life skills, 93
    math, 94
    reading, 83
    writing, 84
  home responsibility inventory, 27
  idea pages
    for Life skills summary, 88
    for math skills summary, 90
    for VIP entries, 70
  math skills demonstration page, 67
  parent letters, 26, 98–99, 105, 118, 130–131
  portfolio covers, 21–25
  portfolio section title pages
    continued, 34
    life skills, 30
    math, 33
    reading, 31
    writing, 32
  reaching your goals, 96
  reading reflections, 126
  reading strategies, 127
  reading survey, 63, 124
  rubrics, 44, 45, 46, 47, 48, 49, 61, 73, 103
  self-monitoring page, 52
  sharing pages, 54–56
  student exit outcomes, 37
  student exit outcomes summary blank, 115
  VIP title page, 35
  visitor information page for creative writing checklist, 77
  visitor log, 29
  writing reflections, 122
  writing sample cover, 76
  writing strategies, 123
  writing survey, 65
  Research paper, student, 32
  Responsibility. *See* Student responsibility
Responsible citizen, 37. *See also* Student responsibility
Résumés, 61
Rewards, 58, 95
Rhodes, L., 2
Romer, R., 6
Room parent, 20. *See also* Parent, duties of room volunteer
Rubrics, 6, 9, 11, 12, 14, 16, 17, 43, 60, 72, 102, 129. *See also* Reproducibles
  definition of, 6, 43
  for biography report, 49
  for classroom behavior expectations, 44
  for interview, 61
  for portfolio expectations, 73
  for reading discussion, 46
  for silent reading expectations, 45
  for silent writing expectations, 47
  for student-led conferences expectations, 103
  for writing discussion, 48
  how to create, 6
  levels for
    emerging, 6, 43
    exceeds standard, 6, 43
    novice, 6, 43
    standard, 6, 43

Safety Patrol, 58
Scheduling. *See* Portfolios; Student-led parent conferences
Schuman, S., 6
Science 1, 4, 7, 9, 11, 14, 17, 32, 37, 50, 70, 113, 135
Sections of the portfolio, 8, 10, 19. *See also* Reproducibles
  life skills, 8, 10
  math, 8, 10
  reading, 8, 10
  writing, 8, 10
  VIP, 8, 10
Self-awareness, 9, 30, 53
Self-concept/self-esteem, 4, 53, 116
Self-confidence, 15, 16
Self-directed learner, 36, 37
Self-evaluation, 13, 30. *See also* Reproducibles; Student self-evaluation; Self-monitoring
Self-monitoring, 9, 30, 36, 50
Self-reflections. *See* Reflections
Self-talk, positive, 30
Semester summary. *See* Student exit outcomes
Sending portfolios home, 16. *See also* Reproducibles
Seven intelligences, 4, 5
Shanklin, N., 2
Sharing pages, 9, 30, 53–56. *See also* Reproducibles

Smith, F., 10, 116
Social studies, 1, 7, 9, 11, 14, 17, 32, 37, 50, 113, 135
  activities, 135
  exit outcomes, and, 37
  writing, and, 32
Society, changes in, 5
Spatial intelligence, 4, 5. *See also* Seven intelligences
Speaking, 37, 41, 88
Special education students, 14
Specials teachers, 14. *See* Art; Music; Physical education
Spelling, 7, 32, 47, 84
Sports, 5, 35, 40, 70, 71. *See also* VIP
Standard, 3, 6, 50. *See also* Rubrics
Standards-based education. *See* Outcome-based education
Standardized tests, 1, 2. *See also* Assessment; Norm-referenced tests; Tests
Stories, student, 2, 3, 7, 74, 84
  drafts of, 32
  final copies of, 32
Strategies, *See also* Reproducibles
  learning 1, 3
  math, 1, 33
  reading, 1, 2, 10, 63, 116, 127
  writing, 1, 10, 65, 123
Student attitudes, 9, 62, 64
Student-centered classrooms, 1
Student evaluations. *See* Student-led parent conference
Student exit outcomes, 9, 10, 11, 12, 16, 17, 21–25, 36, 38, 114, 115, 129. *See also* Reproducibles
  illustrations of by students, 38, 39
  semester summary for, 10, 11, 16, 17, 114, 116, 129
Student initiative, 27
Student interests, 3, 30, 62
Student investment, 10, 13
Student-led parent conferences, 1, 6, 7, 8, 9, 11, 12, 15, 16, 17, 98, 102, 134. *See also* Parent letter; Reproducibles; Rubrics
  agendas, 17, 119, 132
  components of, 11
  confirmation letter for, 104
  decorations for, 12, 15, 109
  explaining to parents/administrators, 14
  fall, 11, 14, 18, 97, 100, 104
  guests in attendance at, 15
  introduction of, 16, 17, 18, 26, 97, 130
  introductions during, 7, 101, 106
  invitations to, 7, 16, 18, 105, 109, 135
  midyear, 10, 11, 14, 117, 119
  parent evaluations of, 11, 108, 118, 136
  preparation for, 14, 15
  questions about, 14, 15
  refreshments for, 7, 12, 15, 99, 107, 109, 131
  rehearsals for, 7, 15, 16, 17, 18, 104, 106
  results of, 6, 7, 15
  room setup for, 107
  schedule for, 7, 14, 15, 99, 100, 109, 131
  spring, 11, 14, 17, 18, 129, 132
  student evaluations of, 11, 16, 17, 18 110, 137
  teacher tips for, 109
  thank you notes, 7, 16, 17, 18, 110, 116, 135
Student motivation, 3, 9, 10, 13
Student ownership, 4, 26, 50
Student pride, 7, 10, 26
Student responsibility, 3, 4, 8, 13, 15, 26, 27, 59, 88, 93
Student self evaluation, 3, 4, 13. *See also* Self-monitoring; Reproducibles
Student self-improvement, 37
Student summary writing. *See* Summary writing
Student supply lists. *See* Supplies
Student surveys, 9, 10, 16, 17
  reading, 62, 63, 124
  writing, 64, 65
Symbols. *See* Visual representations
Synthesis, 30, 31, 32
Summaries, 8, 10, 11, 16, 17, 73, 82, 85, 86, 87, 88, 90, 91, 92, 112, 113. *See also* Example pages for teachers; Student exit outcomes
Supplies, 16, 17
  classroom, 19
  student, 19
Surveys. *See also* Student surveys, Reproducibles

Taylor, P., 3, 4
Teacher effectiveness, 4, 13
Teacher tips, 8, 11, 109
Teacher examples. *See* Example pages for teachers
Teacher summary writing. *See* Summary writing
Teacher supplies. *See* Supplies
Teamwork, 37
Technology, 5
Tests. *See also* Assessment
  Iowa Test of Basic Skills, 1, 116
  IQ, 5
  norm-referenced, 1, 2
  relationship to academic performance, 5
  relationship to real-life tasks, 5
  standardized, 1
Thank you notes. *See* Student-led parent conferences
Thermometer, classroom goal, 10, 12, 95, 96, 112, 116
Thornburg, D., 5
Tierney, R., 1, 2, 4
Time commitment, 13
Timeline, 3, 9, 15–17
  combination, 16
  full school year, 16–17
  modified, 17–18

Title pages for portfolio sections, 8, 9, 11, 16, 17, 19, 28, 112, 113. *See also* Reproducibles
   life skills, 8
   math, 8
   reading, 8
   VIP, 8
   writing, 8
Tradebooks, 2
Twenty-first century, preparation for, 6, 37

Valencia, S., 2, 3
Vandamme, K., 6, 45–48
Very Important to this Person. *See also* VIP
VIP (Very Important to this Person), 8, 9, 11, 14, 16, 17, 21–25, 69, 70, 71, 113
Visitor information page, 72, 74, 77
Visitor log, 8, 9, 11, 21–25, 28
Visual representations, 8, 36, 75, 100, 119, 133
   bar graph, 10, 33, 75
   posters of student exit outcomes, 36
   student illustrations of exit outcomes, 9, 38, 39
   title page cues, 8
   visual clues on agendas, 8, 100
Volunteer work, 59, 70

Wack, B., 9
Whole child, 4, 5, 7, 8, 9, 12, 17
Whole-child portfolios, 1, 4, 5, 8, 11, 12, 14, 15, 16, 17
Work samples, 3, 10
Writing, 1, 2, 3, 4, 8, 9, 10, 12, 14, 16, 17, 37, 47, 48, 112, 113, 120. *See also* Reproducibles; Standard; Strategies; Summaries; Example pages for teachers
   creative writing checklist, 7, 120
   expository/creative/persuasive, 32
   functional, 32
   guidelines for, 10, 12
   reflections, 32, 121, 122
   samples,
      covers for, 76
      evaluation of, 74
      first of the year, 9, 12, 16, 74
      midyear, 12, 16, 17, 113
      end of the year, 10, 12, 16, 17, 120
   strategies, 123
   survey, 9, 10, 16, 32, 64, 65, 120, 121
   workshop, 7

Young Americans Education Foundation, 9, 116

About the Authors

Karen DeLario received her undergraduate degree from the University of Illinois, majoring in elementary education. She earned her master's degree in special education from the University of Northern Colorado.

Karen has taught in the public schools for 21 years. She taught fifth grade in Adams County District #14 for one year. She then taught for twenty years in the Jefferson County School District in fourth grade, fifth grade, and special education. The last two years Karen was a co-teacher with Sue Mundell for the special education inclusion model. Karen is currently on leave from Jefferson County Schools working in real estate at her home in Vail, Colorado.

Sue Mundell is a special education teacher in Jefferson County, Colorado. She received her B.S. from Colorado State University and her M.A. from the University of Northern Colorado. She has worked with students with various disabling conditions for 15 years. Her teaching career has included all grade levels and currently involves the inclusion model through co-teaching with regular classroom teachers.

Regardless of the setting or the abilities of the students, Sue has always advocated the integration of life skills and student responsibility into the curriculum with strong parental involvement. Because of her persistent efforts in these areas, Sue was presented with the Teacher of the Year award in 1993 by the Colorado Council for Learning Disabilities. She continued to the national level as one of eight teachers recognized by the National Council for Learning Disabilities for her commitment to education. This book, *Practical Portfolios*, written with her co-teacher Karen DeLario, exemplifies her belief in integrating student responsibility and parent involvement into a manageable system of classroom goal setting and demonstrated achievement.

www.ingramcontent.com/pod-product-compliance
Lightning Source LLC
Chambersburg PA
CBHW082206230426
43672CB00015B/2916